Before You Start..

Get a *FREE Download* of the
30-page Digital Marketing
Strategy Action Planner

+ Digital Downloads of all
Resources and Templates
inside this book

Implement and execute a clear and effective strategic digital plan. Download all
resources including the Digital Marketing Strategy Action Planner. Go to:

www.ThatActuallyWorks.com/DigitalMarketingPlanner

Companion Guide to
Digital Marketing That Actually Works:
The Ultimate Guide

A practical resource for growing your business online by
using best practices and proven methods that WILL get you
the results you need.

www.ThatActuallyWorks.com/DigitalMarketing
or Amazon: **Digital Marketing That Actually Works: The
Ultimate Guide**

BOOT ★ CAMP
DIGITAL

The **Ultimate** Planner™

Implementing Digital Marketing That Works

ACTUALLY

The Ultimate Planner

**Templates • Quick Start Guides • Checklists
Tip Sheets • Action Planners • and more!**

For general information on our other products and for services or technical support please see www.bootcampdigital.com or Contact Customer Care at 513-223-3878.

ISBN-13: 978-0-9830286-5-9

Printed in the United States of America

First Edition

What's Inside

Step-by-step plan to create a clear and effective digital marketing strategy for your business.

Includes: Digital Marketing Strategy Checklist • Listening Guide • Cascading GSOT • Full Funnel Content Planner • Building Personas Template • Creating Great Content Quick-Start Guide • Creating Great Content Checklist • Content Strategy Template • Social Media Priorities Quick-Start Guide.

Includes: Choosing the Right Social Media Platform for Your Business • Social Media Network Best Practices and Optimization • Digital Advertising Channel Cheat Sheet • Media Plan Evaluation Checklist • Paid Digital Quick-Start Guide • Digital Advertising Strategy OCTO • Facebook Ads Quick-Start Guide • Google Ads Quick-Start Guide • SEO Quick-Start Guide • SEO Tools Tips & Tricks • SEO Keyword Research Quick-Start Guide • Local SEO Quick-Start Guide • Site Speed Quick-Start Guide • Planning Your Website Strategically Quick-Start Guide • What Content Should be on My Website Checklist • Google My Business Quick-Start Guide • Website UX (User Experience) Checklist • Website SEO Quick-Start Guide • Online Reviews Playbook • Email Marketing Quick-Start Guide • Email Marketing Tips & Tricks • Inbound Marketing Quick-Start Guide • Chatbot Marketing Checklist.

Includes: Digital Marketing Measurement Quick-Start Guide • KPI Quick-Start Guide • Benchmarking Quick-Start Guide • Google Analytics Data Analysis Checklist • Google Analytics and Google Tag Manger Quick-Start Guide • ROI Quick-Start Guide • Digital Prioritization Quick-Start Guide • Digital Marketing Strategy 1-Page Planner.

Digital Marketing Strategy
ActionPlanner

Create a clear and effective digital marketing strategy for your business.

What's Inside the Action Planner:

This Digital Marketing Strategy Action Planner will help you to create a clear and effective digital strategy for your business or organization. To make the most out of this guide, consider the following tips:

- ✓ **Don't worry if you don't have all of the answers**. Get as close as you can and move on. Done is better than perfect.
- ✓ **Prioritize the areas that matter most to your business.** Don't complete sections that aren't relevant to you. Focus on what will get you results.
- ✓ **Use a highlighter to highlight the ACTION items** separately from your ideas or insights. This will make it easier for you to plan what you want to do.
- ✓ **Change your plan as needed.** Remember that this isn't set in stone. You can and should learn as you go and adapt. Don't stick to a plan that isn't working.
- ✓ **Think strategy over tactics.** While some tactics or tools might be exciting, always link back to how it contributes to your business goals or objectives.

In the guide, you'll find:

Steps to Building a Digital Marketing Strategy

Building a digital marketing strategy involves 8 clear steps:

1. **Listen and Assess the Landscape**

2. **Clearly Define Your Strategies**

3. **Understand Your Target Audience**

4. **Define Your Content**

5. **Choose the Tools & Tactics to Best Meet Your Needs**

6. **Implement with Excellence and Best Practices**

7. **Track & Measure**

8. **Adjust & Optimize**

This Action Planner will guide you through building a strategic digital marketing plan based on these 8 steps. At the end of this action planner you will have a clear digital marketing strategy for your business.

That being said, it is important to keep your strategy and approach agile to adapt to changes in digital marketing, your customers and to integrate learnings that you have along the way. For this reason, we recommend **revisiting your digital strategy quarterly or semi-annually** to re-think your strategy and adjust as appropriate.

Before you get started, it is helpful to make sure that your digital marketing aligns with the rest of your organization business & marketing strategies. If you have any of the documents below (formally or informally) have them handy as you develop your digital strategy:

- ➤ Business plan or strategy
- ➤ Marketing plan
- ➤ Buyer personas
- ➤ Target audience information

Step 1: Listen and Assess the Landscape

The first step is to listen and assess the landscape. There is more digital data freely available online than more people realize. Listening allows you to learn about your customers, competitors, your business and the category or industry.

A strong digital strategy starts with a clear understanding of what is already happening.

Listen for Your Business/Brand/Company:

Where to Listen:

- **Google Search Results**
- **Google Trends**
- **Google Keyword Tool**
- **Social Networks: Twitter, Pinterest, Instagram, LinkedIn, Facebook, Discussion Forums, Blogs, NicheSites**
- **Community or Industry Sites (based on your category)**
- **Customer service questions/calls/emails**

What are people already saying about your business?

What topics are most asked/discussed or mentioned?

Are any of your current executions effectively driving word-of-mouth?

Overall, what is the sentiment about your business that is discussed online?

Listen to Competitors:

Where to Listen:

- **Search competitors across digital channels**
- **Search engine results**
- **Google trends**
- **Google keyword tool**
- **Social media mentions**

List your top competitors to evaluate (3-5):

What digital channels do your competitors use? (consider all channels – paid, earned, owned)

What are their strategies?

What do they seem to do right? What strategies are working?

What do they seem to do wrong? Where are they missing out?

Listen to the Category or Industry:

Where to Listen:

- **Search engine results**
- **Google trends**
- **Google keyword tool**
- **Social media mentions**
- **Discussion forums**
- **Blogs**
- **Niche industry sites**
- **Industry associations or news sites**

What do people say about the category or industry? What questions do they have?

What content are they interested in related to the industry or category? What questions do people have?

What content is popular? Why?

What are people passionate about related to your industry or category?

What are their pain points related to your category or industry?

What media sites, accounts or people do they look to for advice or to have their questions answered?

Listen to Consumers:

Where to Listen:

- **Google Search Results**
- **Social Networks: Twitter, Pinterest, Instagram, LinkedIn, Facebook, Discussion Forums, Blogs, Niche Sites**
- **Community or Industry Sites (based on your category)**
- **Google Trends**

Where are your consumers online? Where are they open to discussions related to your business or industry?

What are they talking about? What topics resonate with them related to your business?

What topics related to what you do are trending?

What needs and interests do they have related to your product or industry?

Who are some of the top influencers that your target audience follows? Who do they look to for advice or insights?

What words and phrases do they use to discuss your category or industry? What tone of voice do they use? What is the sentiment around it?

Step 2: Defining Your Strategy: GSOT

Define your strategy with the GSOT method – Goals, Strategies, Objectives and Tactics. One of the biggest mistakes in digital marketing is starting with tactics and trying to make them fit into a strategy. Start with your goals and strategies to create a strategic digital plan that drives results.

Define Your Goal

Start by defining your goals – on a high level, what do you want to achieve from your efforts in digital marketing?

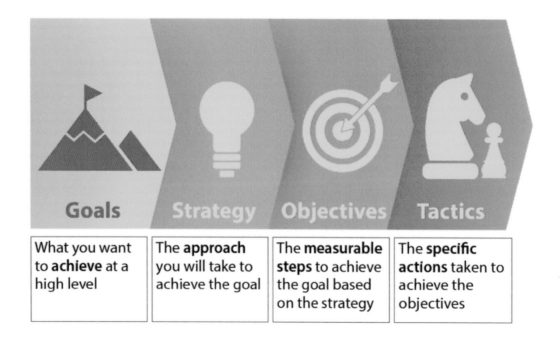

Goals	Strategy	Objectives	Tactics
What you want to **achieve** at a high level	The **approach** you will take to achieve the goal	The **measurable steps** to achieve the goal based on the strategy	The **specific actions** taken to achieve the objectives

NOTE: If needed, brainstorm a list of possible goals and choose one as your primary focus.

Define Your Strategies

You may employ multiple strategies to achieve your goal. Your strategies are the approaches that you use to achieve the goal.

It is helpful to consider your strategies at each stage of the digital path to purchase – ANCRA.

You may choose to focus on one or more areas of the path to purchase. Digital marketing can impact all of these 5 steps.

Start by brainstorming strategies for each step and circle your top 2-4 strategies that you want to focus your efforts around.

Attract/Reach –

Nurture –

Convert –

Retain + Grow –

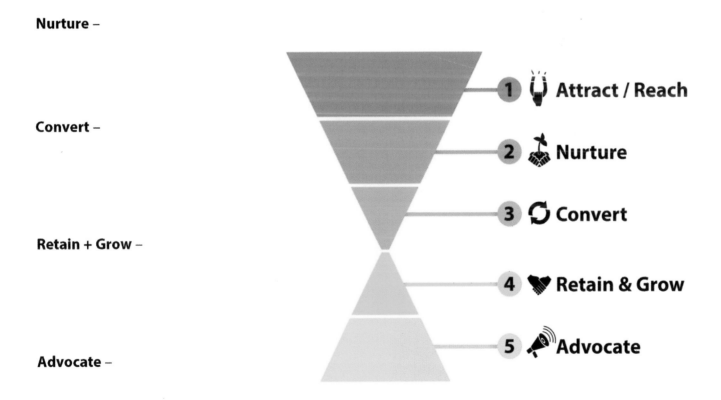

Advocate –

Define Your Objectives

Based on the strategies you selected you'll now want to define your digital marketing objectives. These should be measurable things that you want to achieve as a result of your digital marketing efforts.

Choose approximately 1- 4 objectives for each strategy. Use this space to brainstorm ideas and circle your best ones.

STRATEGY 1 –
Objectives:

STRATEGY 2 –
Objectives:

STRATEGY 3 –
Objectives:

STRATEGY 4 –
Objectives:

NOTE: We will define the tactics at the end of this action planner.

Step 3: Identify Your Target Audience

Clearly identifying your target audience is important since digital marketing allows us to reach audiences much more specific than what is possible in traditional marketing.

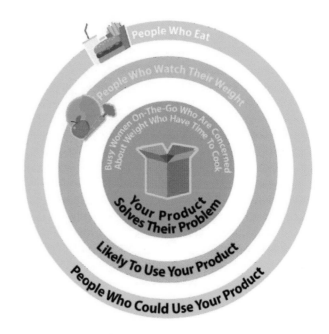

It is important to go beyond demographics when identifying your audience and start thinking about who they really are and why they use your product.

As you look to execute in digital marketing the better you've identified your target the easier it will be to execute.

NOTE: You may have multiple target audiences that you want to reach, which is fine.

Who is your target audience demographically?

What problem do you solve for them?

What are they interested in?

How do they behave online and offline?

Step 4: Define Your Content

Your content strategy should be based on both your business objectives as well as what your audience is actually interested in. Matching up content that achieves both of these is often the key to success in digital marketing.

With an increase in competitiveness for online attention, great (not just good) content is vital to your success. Your content plan should include 3 key items: the topics you will post about, the content formats or mediums you should be prepared to create, and the tone of voice or style guides that are most appropriate for your business or brand. The better you define your content upfront, the easier (and more effective) your digital marketing execution will be.

Content Topics

NOTE: Review your notes from the LISTENING stage to develop your content plan. Consider your target audience, competitors and industry/category in developing an effective plan.

What content is relevant to your business strategies?

What content does your customer/target audience care about?

What content topics overlap the 2 areas? What content is right for your digital strategy? (Aim for 4-8 content topics). You can even include some sample post titles to get started.

TOPIC 1 –
Sample Post Titles:

TOPIC 2 –
Sample Post Titles:

TOPIC 3 –
Sample Post Titles:

TOPIC 4 –
Sample Post Titles:

TOPIC 5 –
Sample Post Titles:

TOPIC 6 –
Sample Post Titles:

Content Mediums

As you look at your content topics, consider the format that your content will take. Will it be text, image or video? A combination of all 3? While your digital marketing tactics will usually define the specific content formats you will create, some of your content may be best suited to different mediums. Consider how you will use the following mediums as a part of your content strategy:

NOTE: You may need to come back to this section after you determine the digital tools that you will use.

Text –

Images –

Videos –

Tone of Voice

Determine the tone of voice and visual style for all of your digital assets.

Visual Assets to Define:

- ✓ Logo
- ✓ Logo variants
- ✓ Fonts
- ✓ Design assets (icon, etc.)
- ✓ Colors
- ✓ Images to use

What is the distinctive voice of your business?

Is your brand serious or funny? In what way? What is or isn't appropriate?

What should your brand sound like online? What type of language should be used?

If your brand had a celebrity spokesperson, who would it be?

Step 5: Define Your Tools and Tactics

Each digital marketing tool that you use should have its own plan for specifically how you will use it and what it will achieve. That being said, it is helpful to step back and think strategically about the digital marketing tools at your disposal and how they can help to achieve your goals.

The Digital Marketing Landscape

As a refresher, the image below represents the digital marketing landscape and top tools/tactics used in each area. It is helpful to consider how each area may fit into your strategy.

Social Media

How can you use each social network strategically to achieve your digital objectives?

Facebook –

Instagram –

Twitter –

YouTube –

LinkedIn –

Pinterest –

Blogs –

Other –

How will you approach building your presence on social media? The primary approaches are Organic, Paid and Community.

How will you build and grow your presence? Whether you are new to a social network or wanting to make your presence more effective it is helpful to evaluate each of the 4Ps.

NOTE: This may be different for each channel that you participate in, and each channel could have a different mix of the three approaches.

<u>Social Network #1</u> –
Approach (Organic, Paid Community):

Plan (Profile, People, Post, Participate):

<u>Social Network #2</u> –
Approach (Organic, Paid Community):

Plan (Profile, People, Post, Participate):

<u>**Social Network #3 –**</u>
Approach (Organic, Paid Community):

Plan (Profile, People, Post, Participate):

Digital Advertising

How can you use each type of digital ad strategically to achieve your digital objectives?

Search Ads –

Social Ads –

Video Ads –

Display Ads –

Define your OCTO for the ad platform that is your biggest priority first.

Objective –

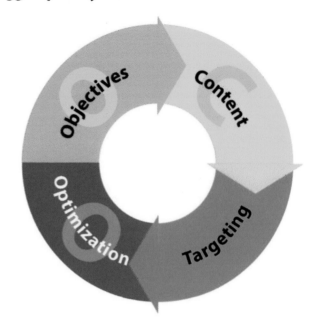

Content –

Target –

Optimization Plan – (what and when will you optimize)

SEO (Search Engine Optimization)

What topics, phrases or keywords do you want to rank for in search engines?

Consider brand, category and affinity. Focus on the most relevant first and then expand once you have success. You may have a strategy for your business overall or for individual products or services.

Brand –

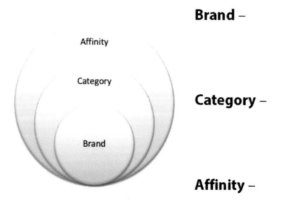

Category –

Affinity –

How will you improve your search rankings for these terms?

Authority (links + shares) –

Power Tip:
Check your links via a backlink checker to see how you compare to competition.

Relevance (content) –

Power Tip:
Check which topics or keywords you need to create content around to rank in search.

Technical (site) –

Power Tip:
Go to www.woorank.com for technical errors and check the Google Search Console.

Website

How does your site currently perform?

Power Tip:
Look at your Google Analytics to understand your current site performance over time.

Site Speed (GTMetrix.com) –

Mobile Friendly (Google Mobile Friendly Test –

Clean and Simple Design?

Content?

Call to Action or Conversions?

Usability or Ease of Use?

What is your website strategy?

Rank in priority order the top 5 things that you want your website to achieve for your business.

1.

2.

3.

4.

5.

How can you improve your website?

Content:

What content is missing? What should be improved? Does this match your SEO strategy for content? Do you need to change/improve your site structure?

Design:

What do you need to improve in the design areas of your site?

Technical:

Do you need to change any aspects to the technical setup of your site?

Conversational Marketing

How can you use each of the following as a part of your digital marketing execution?

Influencer Marketing

Power Tip:
Consider formal and informal approaches to working with industry influencers.

Ratings and Reviews

Power Tip:
Google and Facebook reviews are a great starting point for EVERY business.

Community Management

Power Tip:
Have a plan to respond to comments and questions quickly on social.

Online PR

Power Tip:
Bloggers and online publications can be easy ways to generate PR.

Online Word of Mouth

Power Tip:
Find simple ways to get people talking, or create a specific execution.

Employee Advocacy

Power Tip:
Employees can easily help spread your message if you inspire them ;-)

Email

How can email help to achieve your marketing objectives?

How can you collect email addresses?

Power Tip:
Conduct a touchpoint analysis. Define the value proposition for people to give their email.

How can you drive opens of your emails?

Power Tip:
Remember CURVE: Curiosity, Urgency, Relevancy, Value and Emotion

What ACTION do you want people to take after reading your email?

Power Tip:
EVERY email you send should have a single clear purpose that drives action.

What content will you include in your emails?

Power Tip:
If you are new to email experiment with content and see what resonates.

How often will you send them?

How often will you analyze your email analytics?

CRM

How can a CRM help to achieve your marketing objectives?

Power Tip:
Do you have contact information for customers or prospects? Do you need to manage leads? Do you want to be more targeted? If you answer YES to any of these, you may consider a CRM.

How could you use Marketing Automation to increase conversions of your CRM?

How can you ATTRACT people to your site or content?

How can you ENGAGE people to participate?

How can you DELIGHT them so they want to work with you?

Mobile Marketing

Mobile usage of most digital channels is now greater than computers in most markets. This means that all of your marketing should be optimized for mobile.

Is your digital marketing made for mobile?

- ✓ Social media
- ✓ Digital ads
- ✓ Mobile Search
- ✓ Mobile website
- ✓ Email

Do you have a business reason to create a mobile app?

Are there mobile apps in your industry that your business could partner with?

Are there any existing mobile apps where your business should maintain a presence?

Can Messenger or Chatbots help you achieve your business objectives?

Step 6: Implement

There is almost no end to what you could do in Digital Marketing. The question is where are you most likely to get the best return on your investment. Start by prioritizing the activities and executions that you have identified from each of the digital marketing channels.

Social – Facebook, Instagram, LinkedIn, Twitter, Blogs, YouTube, etc.

Ads – Search, social, video, display, affiliate

SEO – Onsite and offsite optimization

Websites – Landing pages, user experience, testing, conversion optimization, ecommerce

Conversation Marketing – Community management, PR, influencers, reviews, word-of-mouth

Email – Autoresponders, newsletters

CRM – Inbound marketing, lead generation, conversion planning

Mobile – Apps, messaging, optimization

Prioritize Tactics – Hero, Hub, Hygiene

There is almost no end to the digital marketing tactics that you can use to meet your strategic objectives. That being said, we all have limited time and resources.

Use the Hero, Hub, Hygiene model to prioritize your digital activities. Go back to the previous section and prioritize your tactics based on if they are Hero, Hub or Hygiene focused.

Prioritize Tactics – Investment/Impact

Use the investment/impact chart to graph your activities. Be as realistic as possible about both the investment and the size and scope of the impact. Remember the hidden costs, unexpected technical issues and running costs of implementing a digital marketing tactic.

Plot all of your activities on the Investment/Impact graph to further bring clarity to how you can better focus your efforts.

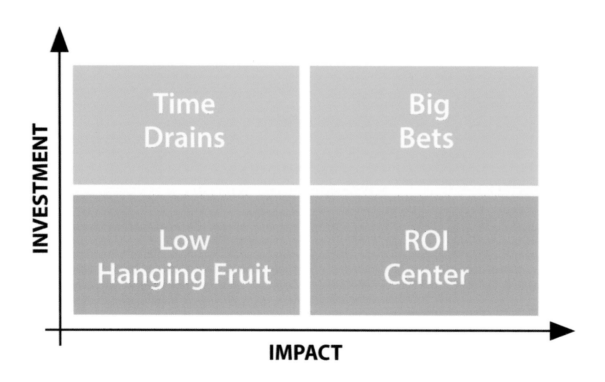

 Power Tip:
Prioritize your plan based on your resources as well. Consider if you will insource or outsource each activity as a part of the prioritization process.

One Page Digital Marketing Execution Plan

My primary **goal** for using digital marketing is:

_____

The digital **strategies** I will use to achieve this goal are:

1) _____

2) _____

3) _____

The people I am trying to reach are:

_____

My Prioritized Plan is:

Immediately –

Short-term (next 3 months) –

Medium-term (3-6 months) –

Long-term (6 months+) –

Step 7: Measurement

Strong measurement starts with strategy. Without knowing WHY you are doing something it is impossible to measure if it is effective. Many issues in digital marketing effectiveness and execution stem from unclear Goals, Strategies and Objectives.

Link your KPIs to your execution – each digital marketing execution should have a clear KPI of what you are trying to achieve and how you will measure success. Remember to set Quantity, Quality and Cost KPIs (or use a single metric that incorporates all of the above).

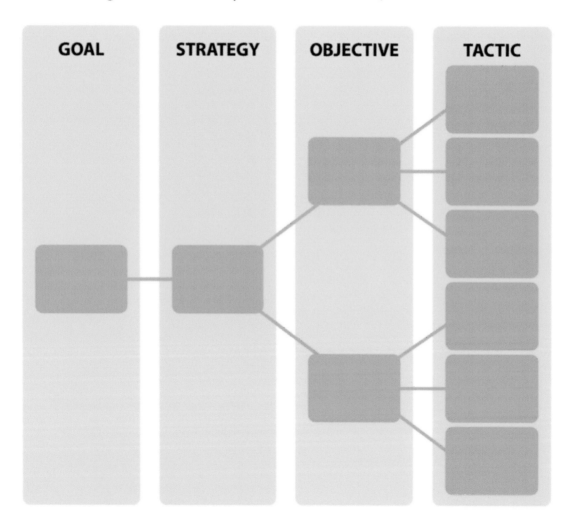

Digital Reporting

Reporting on your results helps you to stay focused and understand if you are getting the results that you expect from your efforts.

What is the purpose of your report?

Who is the audience for your report?

How often will you report?

What are the key metrics to be incorporated into the report?

ROI and Value of Investment

If you have clearly defined KPIs that link back to your business objectives, it often isn't necessary to do additional ROI or value of investment calculations. That being said, for large investments or new ideas it is often helpful to do some type of value analysis to be sure that you are generating sufficient value from your investment.

How can you calculate the value of your investment? Can you compare investments to each other with comparable methodology?

Which investments require a value calculation?

How can you improve ROI for your existing investments? Is this mindset a part of your digital marketing operations?

- Investment:
    - Reduce time spent with tools and processes
    - Reuse and repurpose content
    - Determine what something is "worth" and set a budget

- Return:
    - Test and learn to improve over time
    - Analyze results to grow
    - Increase your reach since your investment in content is fixed

Step 8: Optimization

Optimization of digital marketing is about regularly evaluating your digital marketing efforts and adapting your plan and execution to maximize your results. While reporting usually focuses on sharing results within an organization, analytics and optimization is about the going practice of informally reviewing results and adapting your strategy and execution as needed.

Power Tip:
Even though you have a well thought-out plan – if you aren't getting the results you expect from it you should adapt your plan accordingly. Let results and data guide your decisions.

Build Your Analytics Rhythm

How often will you analyze the results of your digital marketing executions?

What will you look for in your analysis?

Power Tip:
Use the What -> So What -> Now What framework to maximize the impact.

What data sources will you use to validate your assumptions and performance?

What changes can you make based on your results? What changes do you need to seek approval for?

Strategy

Crafting a solid strategy is vital to the success of your digital marketing efforts. This section includes guides and templates to create a compelling strategy that gets results for your business.

Resources Included in this Section:

Having a clear strategy is vital to your success in digital marketing. A clear strategy will link your digital execution to your business goals and objectives and provide value to your customers.

To make the most out of this section, consider the following tips:

- ✓ **Tip 1.** Be clear on what you want to get out of your digital marketing.
- ✓ **Tip 2.** Spend time listening and assessing to gain ideas and insights.
- ✓ **Tip 3.** Develop a strategic content plan to marry execution and strategy.
- ✓ **Tip 4.** Understand your audience as deeply as possible.

1) Listen and Assess the Landscape

- ☐ Conduct a listening audit
  - Per channel ideas/results
- ☐ Develop insights on:
  - Customers, Competitors, Content

2) Marketing Strategy

- ☐ Define a clear, single marketing strategy
  - More is just more.
    FOCUS = RESULTS

3) Target Audience

- ☐ Clearly define a target audience
  - Be as specific as possible – who do you solve a problem for?
- ☐ Define personas to understand all aspects of your target

4) Content

- ☐ Create content "buckets" or topics that are of interest/value to the target audience
- ☐ Content plan (different per channel)
  - Content topics
  - Content type (video, image, text, article, etc.)
- ☐ Content optimized per channel
  - Repurpose and promote content where possible over time

5) Tools

- ☐ Prioritize which social networks to participate in
- ☐ Determine budget, time, and effort for each network
  - Consider if paid strategy is also required.

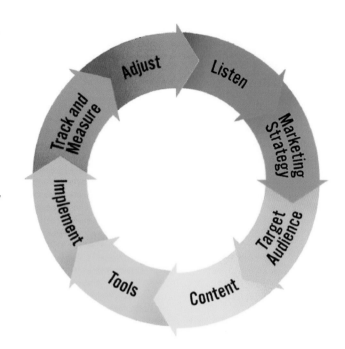

6) Implement

- ☐ Audience building plan
  - Launch
  - Ongoing
- ☐ Management plan
  - Workflows
- ☐ Audience engagement plan

7) Track & Measure

- ☐ Determine relevant KPIs based on marketing objectives
  - 1-2 primary and secondary
- ☐ Establish relevant benchmarks to track performance
- ☐ Build measurement into your workflow

8) Adjust

- ☐ Establish workflow to adapt strategy and tactics as needed
  - Be aware of trends and changes to networks or landscape

The first step in building a digital marketing strategy is to listen and assess the landscape. There is more digtal data freely available online than most people realize. Listening allows you to learn about your customers, competitors, your business and the category or industry.

A strong digital strategy starts with a clear understanding of what is already happening.

Listen to Consumers

Where to Listen:
- Google Search Results
- Google Trends
- Google Keyword Tool
- Social Networks: Twitter, Pinterest, Instagram, Facebook, Blogs, Niche Sites
- Community Sites (based on your category)

Questions to Ask:
- Where are your consumers online?
- What are they talking about?
- What topics related to what you do are trending?
- What needs and interests do your consumers have related to your product or industry?

Listen to Competitors

Where to Listen:
- Search competitors across digital channels
- Search engine results
- Google Trends
- Google Keyword Tool
- Social media mentions

Questions to Ask:
- Define your top 3-5 competitors to evalutate.
- What digital channels do your competitors use? (consider all channels – paid, earned, owned)
- What are their strategies?
- What do they seem to do right? What strategies are working?
- What do they seem to do wrong? Where are they missing out?

Listen to the Category or Industry

Where to Listen:
- Search engine results
- Google Trends
- Google Keyword Tool
- Social media mentions
- Discussion forums
- Blogs
- Niche industry sites
- Industry associations or news sites

Questions to Ask:
- What do people say about the category or industry? What questions do they have?
- What content are they interested in related to the industry or category?
- What content is popular? Why?
- Who are the key influencers?
- What media sites, accounts, or people do consumers look to for advice or to have their questions answered?

Cascading GSOT

GOAL	STRATEGY	OBJECTIVE	TACTIC

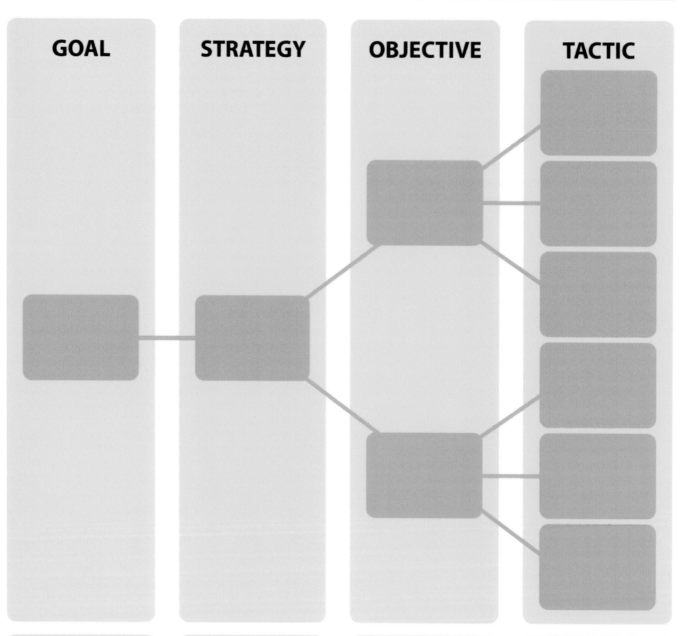

The **GOAL** states what you want to achieve at a high level.

Why are you doing this?

The **STRATEGY** is the approach you will take to achieve this goal.

What is your approach to get results?

The **OBJECTIVE** is a measurable step to achieve the goal based on the strategy.

What do you want to achieve?

The **TACTICS** are specific actions taken to achieve the objective.

How will you achieve it?

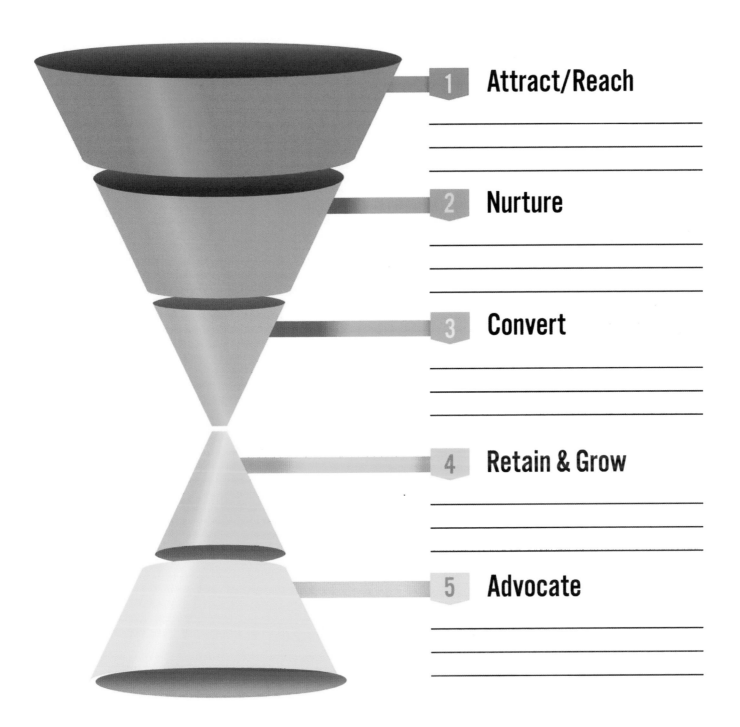

1 Attract/Reach

_____
_____
_____

2 Nurture

_____
_____
_____

3 Convert

_____
_____
_____

4 Retain & Grow

_____
_____
_____

5 Advocate

_____
_____
_____

Persona Template

Name

GOALS
Primary goal? Secondary goal?

CHALLENGES
Primary challenge?

Secondary challenge?

WHAT CAN WE DO
...to help our persona achieve their goals?

...to help our persona overcome their challenges?

What?

BACKGROUND
Job? Career path? Family?

DEMOGRAPHICS
Gender? Age? Income? Location?

IDENTIFIERS
Demeanor? Communication preferences?

HOBBIES & INTERESTS
Hobbies? Interests? Favorite blogs? News sources?

Who?

REAL QUOTES
About goals, challenges, etc.

COMMON OBJECTIONS
Why wouldn't they buy your product/service?

Why?

MARKETING MESSAGE
How should you describe your solution to your persona?

ELEVATOR PITCH
Sell your persona on your solution!

How?

People today have shorter attention spans than ever before. With digital mobile consumption this is increasingly shrinking and we now have shorter attention spans than even goldfish!

In order to combat this you need to craft your message in a smart way. Here are the types of messages that people want and tips to break through the noise so that your content drives results.

Creating Great Content Checklist:

- ☐ My content has a **clear value proposition**.
- ☐ My message is **short, direct and to the point**.
- ☐ My message is **structured for scanning**.
- ☐ My message is **real and authentic**.
- ☐ My content is **interesting**.
- ☐ My message has a clear next step or **call to action**.
- ☐ My call to action can be completed in **as few steps as possible**.
- ☐ I am using **visuals** that illustrate my message.
- ☐ I have considered using **video**.
- ☐ I am using **copy that is catchy**.

What's in it for the person receiving this message? Why should they care?

Is my content easily digestible? Can I break my content down into multiple messages, each with a single focus?

Am I tapping into emotions or using humor? Is my content new and unique compared to everything else?

Are my words capturing the attention of the reader in a clear and memorable way?

50 Types of Digtial Content to Drive More Traffic:

☐ Infographics	☐ Product Reviews	☐ Podcast	☐ Reddit User Creation
☐ Live Video	☐ How-to	☐ Interviews	☐ Content Visualizations
☐ Live Chats	☐ Lists	☐ Research & Data	☐ Media Mentions
☐ Video and Micro Video	☐ E-book	☐ White Papers	☐ Client Testimonials
☐ Guides	☐ Case Studies	☐ Photo Galleries	☐ Inspirational Messages
☐ Blog Posts	☐ Online Events	☐ FAQs	☐ Company News
☐ Newsletters	☐ Q&A	☐ Plug-ins	☐ Company Performance
☐ Mobile Apps	☐ Images	☐ Timelines	☐ Interactive Content
☐ Tweets	☐ Slideshares	☐ Stories	☐ Online Magazines
☐ GIFS	☐ Competitions	☐ Vlogs	☐ Pinterest Posts
☐ Webinars	☐ User-generated Content		
☐ Polls	☐ Personal Opinion Predictions		
☐ Resource Page	☐ Useful Spreadsheets or Documents		
☐ Giveaways	☐ Free Tools or Resoures		
☐ Demos of products	☐ Paid Tools or Resources		

BOOT★CAMP DIGITAL
Check out our intensive Live Digital Marketing Boot Camps and custom corporate training solutions and learn from our accelerated programs. Contact us at 513-223-3878 or info@BootCampDigital.com

Text

- ☐ My content is interesting to my audience.
- ☐ My content is consistent with brand visuals, personality and tone.
- ☐ What I am posting has a singular communication focus.
- ☐ Unnecessary text has been removed.
- ☐ My content includes "bite-sized" messages.
- ☐ My tone is positive.
- ☐ I have prepared a Q&A in advance if I anticipate negative reactions.

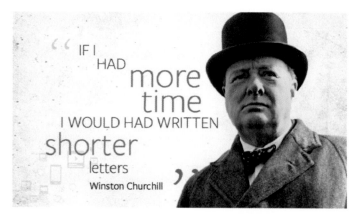

Images

- ☐ I am including visuals.
- ☐ I am choosing images that visually communicate my story.
- ☐ My visuals have a clear focal point.
- ☐ I am applying the rule of thirds.
- ☐ Text in my visuals account for no more than 20% of space.

 Power Tip: Facebook reduces the visibility of images that have too much text.

Video

- ☐ My video shows branding and key communication in the first three seconds.
- ☐ My message is revealed in the first ten seconds.
- ☐ To optimize my video across platforms, I am using a 1:1 square ratio.
- ☐ My message is clear without audio.
- ☐ My video uses fast cuts, and moving images and scenes.
- ☐ My brand is visible for at least half the duration of my video.

 Power Tip: When uploading videos to YouTube, be certain to include all relevant metadata, a catchy title, intriguing thumbnail, and keywords in the description.

Website

- ☐ Design style, language, and navigation is consistent throughout my website.
- ☐ My font is digital-friendly and easy to read.
- ☐ Every page has a clear purpose. What is the goal? What do you want the user to do next?
- ☐ Every page is optimized for search engines.
- ☐ My copy is short, catchy and to the point.
- ☐ When in doubt, I am using proven navigation and design patterns.

 Power Tip: People spend an average of 8 seconds on a homepage.

Landing Pages

- ☐ My landing page has a unique offer.
- ☐ The primary headline on my landing page matches the ad visitors clicked to get there.
- ☐ My call to action (CTA) is big and is positioned above the fold.
- ☐ My landing page has a single purpose and a single-focused message.
- ☐ I am using A/B testing to let my customers decide which message works best for them.
- ☐ I am segmenting my traffic source. My PPC, email, social media, organic and banner traffic have separate landing pages so I can analyze my messaging.
- ☐ I am segmenting my messaging by user type.

About This Template

This template can be used for building a strategy for any type of content. This could be used for social media content, ad content, website content or all of the above.

This template will help you to think strategically about the content that you create and build a clear plan to track and measure the success.

Marketing Objectives

What marketing objectives do you want the content to achieve (be as specific as possible)?

Target Audience

Who is your target audience for the content? Define your audience as specifically as possible based on both demographics as well as behaviors.

Content Brainstorm

Using a variety of online sources, brainstorm a list of possible topics that could fit with your content strategy. Consider a wide variety of ideas by exploring both what people are looking for and what others in your industry are creating.

- Pinterest
- Twitter
- Facebook
- LinkedIn
- Blogs/Forums
- Google Trends
- Google Search
- Industry forums/sites
- Other….

Create Content Buckets

Define the "content buckets" or topics/themes that you will post about. As you create each bucket, consider the 20/60/20 rule as well as Hero/Hub/Hygiene to be sure you have a balanced approach. These approaches will help you to balance the types of content that you create.

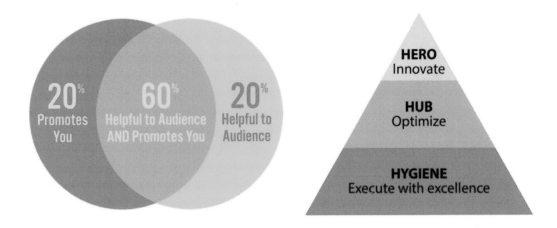

Complete the chart below. *NOTE: You could create one content strategy for all digital content or a separate strategy for each channel.*

A few things to consider:
- Content % should link to marketing objectives
- Evaluate split between promotional and non promotional content
- Consider what your audience is interested in based on the research stage
- Aim for 4-7 content buckets – more than this may become difficult to balance and manage

This is your initial plan. Testing and learning should help you to improve your plan over time as you see what your customers respond to. Be sure to set a cadence for re-evaluating your strategy (monthly, quarterly, etc.) based on learnings.

Content Bucket Template

Bucket/Theme	Marketing Objective	% of Content (add to 100)	Sample Posts
Recipes	Increase consumption	40%	• Gluten free brownies • 10 high protein snacks
Promotional Posts	Drive Awareness of new initiatives	20%	• New flavors • Coupons • New packaging

Content Calendar

The content calendar should define who does what when. It is more detailed vs. the content buckets and should be used to execute against the defined content buckets.

The sample content calendar below can be used for a high-level overview, but you can create something more simple or complex based on your organization needs. This can be created per channel or overall (depending on the complexity of your content strategy). This could also be a full year plan or organized on a monthly/weekly basis.

Blog Posts

What	Monday	Tuesday	Wed	Thursday	Friday	Saturday	Sunday
Post	Top 10 Ab exercises		Avocado toast recipe			Weekend Warrior: Jogging	
Assets Needed	Blog post, image		Blog post, image, video			Blog post, image	
Time	1:00 pm		3:30 pm			1:00 pm	
Owner	Kelly		Sarah			Bill	
Promotion Plan	$XX ad spend		$XX ad spend + schedule on all social networks 1X/year			$XX ad spend + schedule on all social networks 1X/year	

What	Monday	Tuesday	Wed	Thursday	Friday	Saturday	Sunday
Post							
Assets Needed							
Time							
Owner							
Promotion Plan							

Content Workflow

To deliver your content calendar, create a workflow outlining the process and approvals to deliver content each month/week/quarter (based on your work cycles).

In the space below, draw out your content workflow starting from the "content live" date.

Day 0 – Content Live

Content Promotion

If you have great content build a plan to re-promote your best content to get the most "bang for your buck". Consider all available means (Paid, Earned, Owned) to drive your content and using the space below draw out your plan to re-promote your best content.

Note: This works best for "evergreen" content, or content that isn't outdated based on time. For example, "10 Ab Exercises is always relevant (evergreen) but "10 Ways to Get Bikini Ready is maybe only relevant in the Spring and can only be re-promoted in the Spring of each year.

Content Testing

Create a proactive testing plan to continuously optimize your content.

5 Things I Want to Build Tests for:

1.

2.

3.

4.

5.

Content Analysis

How frequently will you analyze your content?

What trends/patterns will you look for?

Why Social Media?

1 in every 5 minutes online is spent on social media – and this number is only growing. As people spend more and more time on social media it becomes a more relevant place for you to connect with your customers and build awareness for your business. Social media allows you to:

- ✓ Build awareness for your practice
- ✓ Generate word-of-mouth
- ✓ Build deeper connections with patients
- ✓ Humanize your business
- ✓ Generate new patients

What it Takes

While social media can be an exciting way to connect with existing customers, generate new customers and build your business presence, it is important to understand the time and effort involved. For each social network you should estimate:

- ☐ Learning the network, exploring businesses: 4 – 8 hours
- ☐ Setup time: 2 – 4 hours
- ☐ Creating content: 1 hour/week
- ☐ Monitoring & Responding: 5 – 10 minutes a day

Make sure that you have the time to setup and manage a social network. Having social networks that aren't active can work against you as people expect you to be active and respond.

Social media execution can often be managed by an office manager – make sure that they understand basic best practices and the vision for your business so that you represent yourself well online. You can also do much of the management from a mobile phone, making it more efficient.

 Power Tip: *The businesses that do this best (without too much effort) build social media into their day-to-day practice. They look for opportunities to take photos or share videos and tips in their daily activities.*

Steps to Getting Started

Businesses often make the mistake of starting by setting up a Page with no clear plan. Building a plan (even informally) upfront will help to ensure your success.

1. **Look, Listen and Learn** – Explore how other businesses are using it. What is generating interest? What doesn't work well? Learn how people and businesses use the network.

2. **Define your Objectives** – Clearly define what you want to achieve with your presence. Are you aiming to strengthen relationships with existing customers and drive referrals or connect with new customers?

3. **Determine your Target Audience** – Being clear about who you want to reach and knowing some of their demographics will help you to make stronger connections. Often connecting with existing customers is a strong starting point. Consider who your typical demographic is that you want to reach on the social network.

4. **Create your Presence** – Determine which social network makes the most sense for you based on your goals and target audience. Create your Page or Profile (be sure to use a consistent username and visuals on all networks).

5. **Build your Content Plan** – Determine what you will post about (the topics), the types of posts (videos, pictures, etc.) and how often you will post. Think about what is interesting or remarkable that your target audience would be interested in. Customer questions can be a great source of inspiration. Determine who will be responsible for creating the content (depending on your business it could be you or an office manager), and remember that you can post directly from your phone.

6. **Manage and Connect** – You can schedule out your posts in advance or rely on day-to-day inspiration. You'll also want to reply to comments or questions and connect with others. You can set up social networks to receive notifications and decide who will respond. You may want to get involved personally for negative or sensitive comments. Most new small business pages only get a handful of comments a week.

7. **Analyze and Improve** – It isn't good enough to just post. Make a point to do a monthly "check-in" to evaluate what works, what doesn't work and if you need to adjust your plan based on results.

Channels

With so many social channels, businesses must focus on impact. Spend time where you will have the most impact and implement best practices to get better results faster.

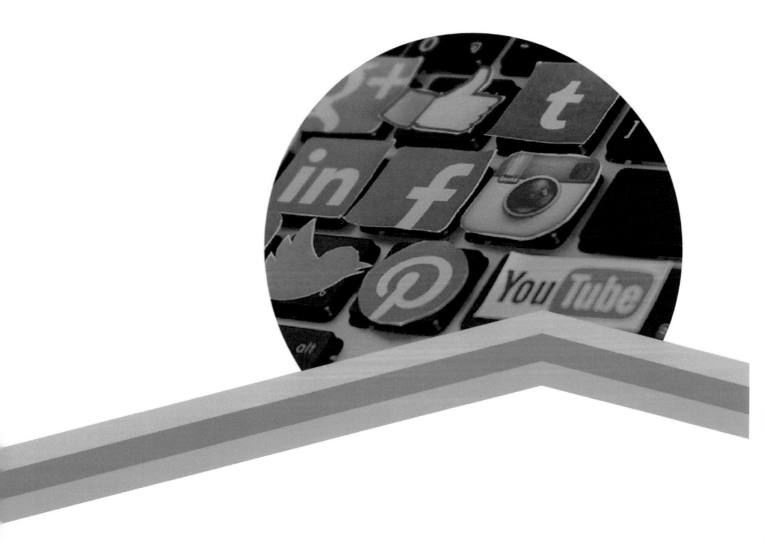

Resources Included in this Section:

When it comes to digital marketing, the key to success is to determine which tools are most likely to drive your business forward and then implement with excellence. These resources will help you understand digital marketing tools and best practices to grow your results.

To make the most out of this section, consider the following tips:

- ✓ **Tip 1.** Do fewer things better – don't take on too much.
- ✓ **Tip 2.** Optimizing your existing tools can grow ROI faster than new tools.
- ✓ **Tip 3.** Be sure to use best practices – the devil is in the details.
- ✓ **Tip 4.** Know what matters most for your business strategy and #ThinkImpact

	Facebook	Instagram	Twitter	YouTube	LinkedIn	Pinterest	Snapchat
USERBASE	**2.2** billion users	**1** billion users	**330** million users	**1** billion users	**250** million active users	**200** million users	**200** million users
GENDER	**53%** Women	**51%** Male	**53%** Male	**62%** Male	**56%** Male	**71%** Women	**70%** Women
AGE	Most common age demographic **25 - 34**	55% of people **18 - 29** use Instagram	35% of users are between **18 - 29**	26% of users are between **35 - 44**	27% (81 million) of users are between **30 - 49**	Most common age demographic **25 - 34**	**7/10** users are millenials
INCOME & EDUCATION	**72%** of online users with an income of $75k+ use Facebook	**63%** of users earn over $50k	**56%** of users earn over $50k	**46%** of users earn over $75k	**44%** of users earn over $75k	**57%** of users have a four-year college degree	**62%** of users earn less than $50k
GREAT FOR	A variety of industries and businesses and B2C Marketing	Demonstrating brand culture • Engaging young audiences • Showing Products	Thought leadership • Trending topics • News, culture, and events	How-to • Product reviews • Gaming • Entertainment • Education	B2B Marketing • Recruiting • Networking	Retail sales • Fashion, DIY, Home, Beauty, and Food • Showing Products	Reaching young audinces • Showcasing products & lifestyle
IDEAL CONTENT	Images & Videos	Images & Videos	Text, Links, GIFs, Short Video	Video	Short Blogs, Infographics, Images & Videos	Images, Infographics	Video
ADVERTISING	Solid – Best in the business	Excellent, courtesy Facebook	Decent	Robust platform High ROI	Strong – ROI not up to the mark	Good if targeted well	Expensive
DRAWBACKS	Clickbait & Fake News	Limited user attention span	Lack of security against trolls and abusers	Videos can be expensive to make	Largely focused on careers and jobs	Very niche demographics	Advertising is expensive • Conent self-destructs • You cannot comment/like posts

	Facebook	Instagram	Twitter	YouTube	LinkedIn	Pinterest	Snapchat
POSTING FREQUENCY	1-4x per week	1-7x per week	2-10x per day, including retweets & replies	Weekly or when applicable	1-7x per week	3-14x per week	4-7x per week
WHEN TO POST	When relevant to audience	When audience is online	Spread throughout the day	When audience is online	During business hours	Spread throughout the day	When relevant to audience
USE OF HASHTAGS	Limited search functionality. Recommended: 1-2 per post	Recommended: 20-30 per post	Recommended: 1-2 per tweet	Use in descriptions. Recommended: a handful per upload	Recommended: 1-5 per post	Recommended: 3-5 per post	Not popularly used
BEST PERFORMING CONTENT	Photos · Videos	Photos · Short videos	Questions · Multimedia	Product Reviews · How-to Guides · Educational videos	News · Updates · Articles	Style · Home · Food & Drink · Beauty	Fun & playful · Lenses & filters
IDEAL VIDEO LENGTH	1 Minute for video 5+ Mins for Live video	30 Seconds	45 Seconds	2 Minutes	1-2 Minutes	Based on source video	10 Seconds
CONTENT TIPS	Thumb-stopping power · Short & catchy videos & images · Respond to comments	Real photos of real things · Use hashtags · Single focus of image	Mix content · Retweet · Reply and participate	Clear purpose for video · Compelling storyline · Add variety to video topics	Positive & relevant content · Add images & video · Value for audience	Variety of content · Create multiple boards · Curate content from other sources	Capture attention · Showcase business or product · Fun & light
AUDIENCE BUILDING TIPS	Post Consistent and engaging content · Boost posts	Use hashtags · Engage with audience	Tweet more often · Use hashtags and participate	Optimize for search · Post consistently	Add contacts to your network · Engage via comments and groups	Post often · Create searchable descriptions	User-generated content · Cross-promote on other platforms

Choose Your Channel Strategically

Link your media channel to your marketing strategy and choose the channel that will maximize your return.

Channel	Awareness	Nurture	Convert	Retain/ Advocacy
Display/ Programmatic	Inexpensive reach	Views may be more passive, less involved	Typically low click rates	Inexpensive reach with retargeting options
Search ads	More expensive per click for top-of-funnel awareness	Connect with interested in category	Connect with motivated searchers	Expensive way to reconnect with customers
YouTube	Longer video views (6 second bumpers inexpensive)	Longer video views (True-view ads)	Few people click	Depends on objective
Facebook	Inexpensive reach (although short view times)	Need thumb-stopping content to drive longer views	Efficient conversions with right call to action	Retargeting and broad reach
Instagram	Inexpensive reach (although short view times)	Stories can drive longer view times	Instagrammers less likely to change tasks	Retargeting and broad reach

Power Tips:
- ✓ Build sufficient results on one channel before adding more
- ✓ Consider targeting options per channel and how that impacts your strategy
- ✓ Consider most appropriate formats for each channel & strategy
- ✓ Evaluate channel/format for reach/going advertising vs. high-impact campaigns
- ✓ Optimize creative for the channel

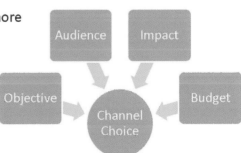

GOAL: Optimize for media results and impact. Remember that not all channels or formats are equal.

Goal = Maximize the objective with the target audience for the budget.

Media plans are customized based on:

- ☐ Objectives – What you want to achieve
- ☐ Target Audience – Who you want to reach
- ☐ Budget – What you can afford

A strong media plan should balance:

- ☐ Objective – What you get
- ☐ Impact – How impactful is the medium and format
- ☐ Cost – Optimized for objectives and audience
    - ☐ Remember: Not all channels have equal impact

The plan should include:

- ☐ Timing (also time of day insights)
- ☐ Objective
- ☐ Buying method
- ☐ Format
- ☐ Targeting
- ☐ Creative needed
- ☐ Budget
- ☐ Planned result
- ☐ KPI
- ☐ Benchmark

Making the most of your budget:

- ☐ Maximize one channel before adding more
- ☐ Aim to reach 15% of target audience with each creative
- ☐ Reduce creative (if needed) to maintain impact
- ☐ Balance working and nonworking budget
- ☐ Aim for unique reach when adding channels
- ☐ Use always on to maintain brand (too little = flights) (too much = redistribute)

Questions to answer in review:

- ☐ What is the rationale behind the channel selection?
    - ☐ Link to: Objective, Target Audience, Budget
- ☐ Are the formats right for the Objective, Audience and Budget?
- ☐ Does each creative/campaign have sufficient budget?
- ☐ How many creatives are needed? (balance working and nonworking)
- ☐ How does the plan compare to benchmarks?

Digital Advertising

Digital advertising is one of the biggest areas of digital marketing and accounts for most marketing dollars. Digital has eclipsed traditional in marketing budget spending and is projected to continue to grow. This isn't surprising as consumers spend more time on digital devices vs. traditional media. Digital advertising is so cost effective that even small businesses can afford it vs. other traditional methods of advertising. Digital advertising increases awareness for your business in a more cost-effective way than traditional.

Primary Types of Digital Ads

Digital advertising has many forms and formats and includes both mobile and desktop advertising. The primary types of digital ads are:

- **Search** – Search engine ads appear around search engine results and are usually used to drive motivated buyers to your website. Google Ads (AdWords) is the most popular platform for search ads.
- **Social** – Social Media ads are displayed on Facebook, Instagram, Twitter, LinkedIn and other social networks. They usually have very detailed targeting.
- **Display** – Display ads appear around content online, like news sites, in games or on blogs. There are many different creative formats that can be used in display. You can also buy display ads through the Google Ads platform.
- **Video** – Video ads are predominantly displayed on YouTube, although video as a format can be used on all advertising platforms (except search).

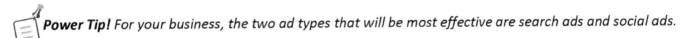

Power Tip! For your business, the two ad types that will be most effective are search ads and social ads.

How Digital Ads are Bought

Typically, digital ads are purchased through an auction-based bidding system in a pay-per-click (PPC) model. You set a maximum cost per click that you are willing to pay, and a budget.

In most bidding systems ads that have high user value (people like them and interact) are able to pay a lower cost. The ad platforms like Facebook and Google want to encourage you to create ads that give a good user experience.

Getting Started with Digital Ads

You are most likely to get the best results through search ads on Google and Facebook Ads. Google ads show up at the top of search engine results. Facebook Ads appear as sponsored posts in the news feed, or on the right side of the page. Depending on your budget, start with Facebook Ads and then Google Ads. Measure your results so you know if your ads are worth the investment.

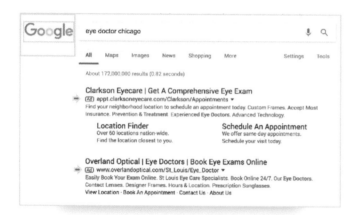 

Steps to Building an Effective Advertising Plan

Facebook Ads and Google Search Ads are most effective overall at driving results for businesses. Follow these steps and tips to maximize your results in each network. Prioritize based on what will have the biggest impact for the least amount of investment.

1. **Strategy**
   Link your media channel to your marketing strategy and choose the channel(s) that will maximize your return.
   - Facebook Ads
     - Great for driving awareness, inexpensive
     - Efficient at converting patients to take an action
     - Effective at driving a broader reach through existing patients
     - Good for retargeting users by showing content to those who have already interacted with your website
   - Google Ads
     - Search ads on Google are best for connecting with motivated searchers and converting them to take an action. For example, an ad with a call to action to schedule an appointment.

- Google Ads may also be a good way to nurture potential customers who are still researching options and have not yet made a decision.

2. Target
- Facebook Ads – Cost effective as it allows you to target specific interests and behaviors.
- Google Ads – Target by geographic area.

3. Channel
In general, Google Ads are going to cost more than Facebook Ads. Test and learn to determine which channel is best at driving results. You may determine that both channels are effective at driving similar or different results. For example, you may discover that Facebook is great for driving awareness, but Google drives new customer sign ups, or you may find that both are effective at driving new customers.

4. Format
- Facebook Ads – Image ads perform better than text only ads, and video performs better than images.
- Google Ads – Search ads are text only format.

5. Creative
Your creative should align with your business objective and effectively drive engagement.

 Power Tip! *Search for your competitors or other businesses like yours in different cities for ideas and inspiration for the types of ads that they are running.*

6. Buy
Determine your budget. What is the expected impact or result? What is the estimated revenue that you will gain? Your budget should align with this.

7. Optimization
Test different variables in your ads. Test different ad text, calls to action, and contents of your images.

8. Analysis
This is the key to effective optimization. Analyze your data to determine what works best at driving results. Use these insights to decide where and how much to invest.

Objectives

Consider the objective for your digital ad. **What do you want the ad to achieve for you?** Each ad can only have one objective, so it is important that you choose wisely. Choosing the right ad objective is important because once that decision has been made, the other parts of the ad will be pre-defined based on it.

Content

What is the right content to connect with your target audience and reach your marketing objectives? Balancing content that people are interested in with content that achieves your goals is the key to success.

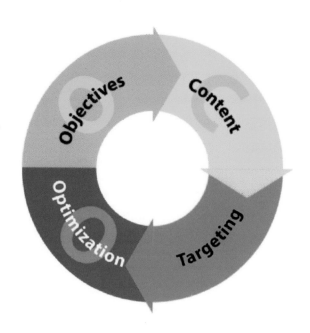

Targeting

Once your ad objective is selected you can choose your target audience. Define your audience as specifically as possible, and don't be afraid to create multiple ads aimed at multiple target audiences.

Optimization

Optimizing your digital ads is vital to your success and is one of the things that make digital ads such a powerful marketing tool. **Plan to optimize.** Build testing in to your digital marketing plan. Test different ad formats, content and targets to discover what works best for you.

Complete the chart below to link your Ad Objective to your Target Audience to your Content. Each level should flow from the one above: For example, your target audience(s) should be based on your objective and your ads (content) should be specific to your target audience.

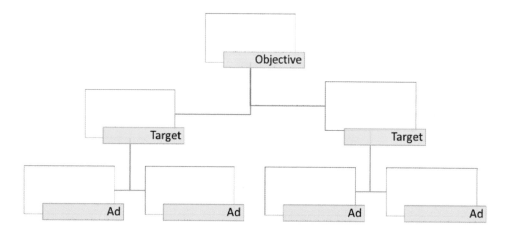

Why Facebook Ads?

Facebook ads are one of the best and most cost-effective ways to reach audiences online. Without advertising, it is now increasingly unlikely that people will see your content on Facebook, so ads are a growing part of most Facebook strategies.

Getting Started with Ads

It is easy to get started with Facebook ads – all you need is a Facebook Business Page and a credit card.

- Spend as little as $1/day on each ad
- The self-serve platform makes it easy to get started DIY or have transparency if hiring an agency
- You can test and receive immediate results on how your ads are performing
- To get started, visit https://www.facebook.com/adsmanager/ and click Create Ad.

Choose Your Ad Objective

Start by choosing the Facebook advertising objective that best matches what you want to achieve.

Facebook regularly adds new objectives as they evolve to better meet the needs of advertisers. Starting with what you want to achieve will make your other decisions (targeting, format, content) easier to make.

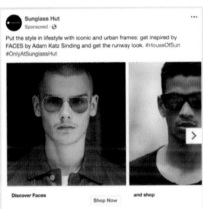

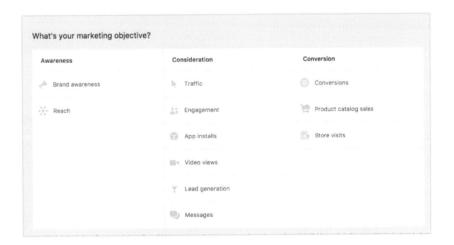

Here are a few objectives and actions to consider:

Objective: Awareness

Run a "likes" campaign to increase your overall visibility and awareness of your business and what you offer. Less than 1% of your fans will see your organic (non-paid) content, so investing in growing your network will help you earn organic visibility over time. Choose the "Engagement" objective, then "Page Likes".

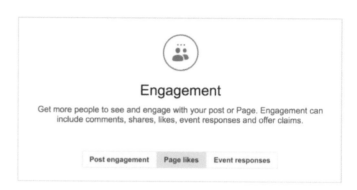

Objective: Booked Appointments (Traffic)

Run a campaign to guide traffic to the page on your site where customers can schedule an appointment. Choose the "Traffic" objective and link your ad to your online scheduling page of your website.

Facebook Targeting

Facebook targeting is one of the things that makes it most unique. Consider how you can use each type of targeting to specifically reach the right person with the right message.

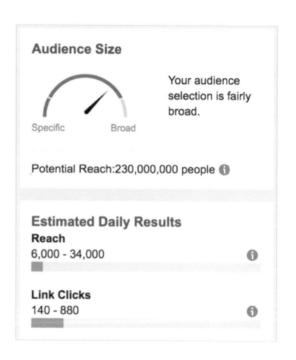

Facebook targeting impacts your budget. Pay attention to the Audience Size and Estimated Daily Results as you adjust your targeting options. Keep your objectives in mind as well, to help you estimate the potential return on your investment. If it costs too much to make a small number of people aware of your business, your targeting may need adjusted.

Custom Audiences

- **Email/phone lists** – you can upload an existing email or phone list and Facebook will cross reference that list with their database. Any matches will be added to a custom audience that you can then show your ads to. This option is great for targeting existing customers in your list and reminding them of current offers or specials. Just be mindful of the messaging so it comes across in a way that is relevant and adds value, not in a way that makes them feel that their privacy has been violated.

- **Website retargeting** – show ads to people who have visited your website. You will need to add some code to your website, called a Facebook pixel. This is a great way to stay top of mind with customers and potential customers who have already visited your site.
- **Lookalike audiences** – build a larger audience by targeting users who have similar attributes as your existing audience.

 Power Tip! *The magic number for custom audiences is around 1000. Building custom audiences work best if you have an email/phone list with at least 1000 matches, or a source list of at least 1000 to build your lookalike audience.*

Demographic + Location
- Get as specific as zip codes to include or exclude people.
- Age, gender and more available
  - Life events (recently moved, parents, etc.)

 Power Tip! *Consider targeting customers with life events that align with the services you offer. For example, eye exams are often needed for children who enter a new school. Therefore, if you are an eye doctor, you could target people who have recently moved and have children of a certain age.*

Interests and Behaviors
- Countless options based on interests in topics on and off Facebook.
- Musical tastes, food, work, hobbies and more.
- Behaviors based on various factors: engaged shoppers, etc.

 Power Tip: *Focus first on targeting the audience that best aligns with your primary target audience. As your skill set improves with ads, you can add other more specific or segmented target audiences for Facebook Ads so each group receives a message that seems customized for them!*

Facebook Ad Formats
Facebook offers many different ad formats to reach your audience including video, images, links and more. You can create an ad by clicking "Create Ad" or promote existing content by clicking "Boost Post" on an existing post.

 Power Tip! *Ads that you create, and boosted posts both appear in the news feed as a sponsored post. Creating an ad will give you a few additional features than you would have by clicking "Boost Post". However, the Boost Post feature is a quick way to promote a post and get more visibility.*

Standard Formats

Photo – Use beautiful images to convey your message.

Video – Use motion to tell your story and draw customers in.

Carousel – Show multiple photos or videos in a single ad.

Slideshow – Create a lightweight video ad from images.

Collection – Tell your story with a single ad showing multiple products.

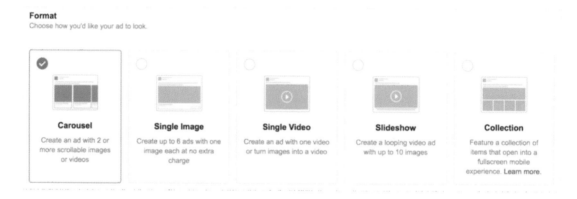

Objective Specific Formats

Lead Ads – Collect information about your audience right on Facebook.

Dynamic Ads – Customize your ad specifically for the patient you are reaching.

Link Ads – Drive traffic to your site to draw people in.

Facebook Ad Content

Regardless of your ad type, you need content that your audience is interested in. On Facebook you only have a few seconds to grab attention. Successful Facebook ads usually follow these best practices:

- **Single message**
- **Thumb-stopping power (Grabs attention in the first few seconds)**
- **Focused visual or video**
- **Relevant to the audience**

How Much Do You Pay for Ads?

Facebook ads are bought and sold through an "auction" system, which means that there isn't a set price for an ad. Ad pricing is based on supply (how many people in your target audience are on Facebook) and demand (how many people want to reach that audience), as well as how good the ad is.

- How much you are willing to pay
- How narrow your target audience is (you often pay more for more specific targeting)
- How good your ad is (user value)

1. Auction

If people don't seem to like your ad you will have to pay more for people to see it.

You can buy Facebook ads in different ways depending on your ad objective. For example you can choose to pay for:

- Impressions
- Reach
- Clicks
- Leads generated
- Conversions
- Video Views

Facebook will give you an estimate of what you should expect to pay once you have setup your ad. You can also set maximums as well as daily and/or lifetime caps to control your budget. Many local businesses get results by spending as little as $1 a day. Ultimately, your budget should result in a positive return on your investment.

Facebook Ad Optimization

Once an ad starts to run the results are visible immediately. Unlike traditional advertising you don't have to wait until the end of a campaign to see what works. You can test, learn and optimize as you go.

- Test different ad copy (images, videos, text)
- Test targeting options
- Test different bidding choices
- Try different ad objectives

Build a testing plan upfront so you can see what really works for you and continue to improve your ROI (return on investment).

What Are Google Ads?

Google ads show up at the top of search engine results when someone is searching. Google Ads (formerly AdWords) is a Pay Per Click platform, meaning the advertiser pays a certain amount each time their ad is clicked.

Why Google Ads?

Google Ads is still one of the best ways to reach your audience online where they are searching. Consider these stats:

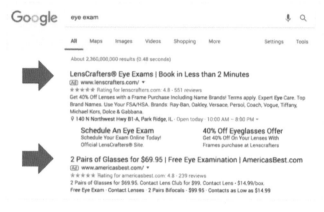

- 86% of consumers use the Internet to find a local business.
- Google owns 71% of the search market share.
- About 25% of the clicks on Google go to the ads.
- 89% of the traffic generated by search ads is not replaced by organic clicks when ads are paused. Studies show that click through rates are higher on both paid and organic search results when both are present. Running PPC ads can build credibility and brand awareness, and can result in a higher click through rate.

Getting Started with Google Ads

It is easy to get started with Google Ads – all you need is a Gmail account and a credit card.

- Sign up at: https://ads.google.com/
  - Choose your goal: "Get more visits to your physical location".
  - If you already have a Google My Business listing, you can connect to it here.
- You can test and receive immediate results on how your ads are performing
- Campaigns are setup with one or more ad groups.
- Set a budget. Most businesses have a marketing (ad) budget between 3 and 5 percent of their anticipated yearly revenue. Google Ads would be a portion of that overall budget.

Step 1: Setup A Campaign + Ad Group(s)

Campaigns can be used to organize categories of products or services that you offer. You will set your overall budget at the campaign level.

Here's what you need to know about each campaign setting:

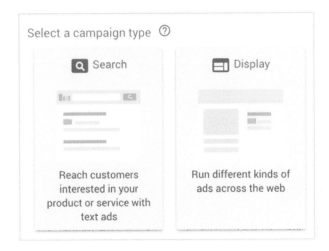

- **Campaign Name** = Only visible to you. Use this to clearly label your campaigns so it's easy to find.
- **Campaign Type** = Choose a campaign goal that aligns with your overall objective such as website traffic or brand awareness. You will also be asked to choose a campaign type. Choose search network for standard PPC text ads. You may also choose display network if you would like to run display ads on other sites.
- **Networks** = Set where you would like your ads to appear. For the search network, you can choose to show your ads on Google search sites and search partners.
- **Devices** = You can target your ads to show on desktop, tablet and mobile devices. Consider running ads on all devices.
- **Locations and languages** = Be sure to target the geographic area you serve. You can set this by city, zip code, etc.
- **Bidding and budget** = Set a bid limit, which is the most you'll pay for each click. Your budget set to an average daily amount. Google will show estimated traffic for your budget so you have an idea of how far your dollars will go. You can adjust your budget at any time.
- **Ad Extensions** = Include additional information in your ads, such as your business address, links to specific pages on your website such as your appointment scheduler or a specials page, and your phone number.
- **Additional Settings** = You can set a campaign start/end date, schedule your ads to show only on certain hours of the day or days of the week and more.

Ad groups within your campaigns contain one or more ads which target a set of keywords. For example, you may have a Campaign for Eye Exams and within the campaign you have an Ad Group targeting eye

exams for kids (and related keywords) and an Ad Group targeting eye exams for adults. Organize your ad groups by theme and aim to add around 20 keywords to each ad group.

*📝 **Power Tip!** Google Ads has a built in Keyword Tool which can be found by navigating to the Tools Icon, then choose Keyword Planner. Enter a keyword phrase like "eye exams" to discover other related terms, average monthly search traffic, and competitiveness.*

Step 2: Setup Ads & Extensions

Once you've signed up and created your first campaign and ad group, you can start creating ads. To effectively reach potential customers, your text ads should be informative, relevant, and engaging. Here's what you need to know about creating text ads.

Google Search Ads Formats

Here are the basic elements of a search ad and tips for how to create great ads. The exact character limits and image sizes may change. When you are setting up an ad, Google will tell you the current character limits.

Headline – Consider using keywords that people are searching for. Data shows that click through rates are higher on ads that include the search term. The Google Keyword Planner Tool is a great tool to discover what people are searching for.
Description – Include a call to action in your description.
Display URL – This shows your website address, and you can add more descriptive words to the URL to help users understand what to expect when they click.

Google Ad Content

Regardless of your ad type, you need content that your audience is interested in. Only about 25% of all Google searchers will click on the ads at the top or bottom of a page, so you need to grab their attention. Successful Google ads usually follow these best practices:

- ✓ Single message
- ✓ Relevant to the audience
- ✓ Grabs attention
- ✓ Clear call to action
- ✓ Include target keywords in your ad copy

In these examples, the "Good" example checks all of the boxes, while the "Bad" example doesn't.

Good

Do You Need An Eye Exam? | See The Difference Right Away
Ad　www.eyeexamcenter.com/eye/exams

Affordable Eye and Vision Exams. Call Us Today For An Appointment.

Bad

Optical Exam | Make Appointment | Check Out Our Contact Styles
Ad　eyeexamsforyou.com/discount/doctor

An eye examination is a series of tests performed by an ophthalmologist, optometrist, or orthoptist. You can get your test here and we have special colored contacts for Halloween.

Ad Extensions

You can choose to show additional business information with your ad, such as your address, phone number, or links to specific pages on your site. To add extensions, navigate to Ads & extensions, then click Extensions at the top of the page. Click the icon to view the options available.

Step 3: Choose Keywords

To reach potential customers, think of the words that they are searching for. If you're not sure, Google Ads can help. Navigate to Keywords on the left and click the icon to add your keywords. Enter a search term (such as "eye doctor" or "eye exams") to view related keywords and average monthly traffic. Click the keyword to add it to your Ad Group.

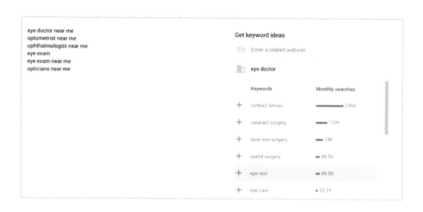

 Power Tip! *By default, the number of average monthly searches is for the entire US. Actual traffic in your geographic area is just a percentage of this total. The idea here is to discover popular keyword searches.*

 Power Tip! *Keep in mind that more competitive keywords can also cost more and could potentially use up your budget quickly. Use the Google Keyword Planner to identify competitiveness and average cost per click. Choose less competitive/lower cost keywords to help control your budget.*

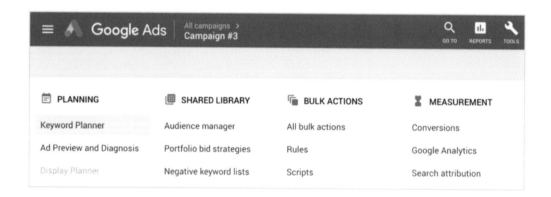

You can also use the Google Keyword Planner to explore keywords and add them to your Ad Group.

1. Navigate to Tools > Keyword Planner
2. Choose "Find new keywords" and add a few keywords to start (i.e. "eye doctor" and "eye exams").
3. Select keywords and click "Add to plan".

4. Click "Plan overview" on the left to view estimated results and budgets. Explore changing the settings here such as max cost per click or moving the blue dot on the graph to see how much you can expect for different budget settings.

CPA = Cost Per Acquisition
CTR = Click Through Rate
CPC = Cost Per Click

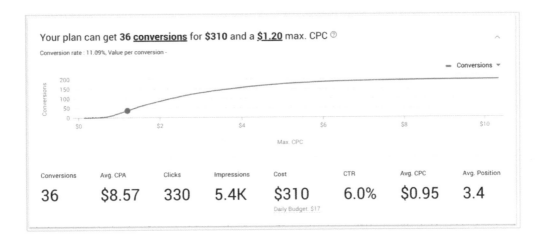

Step 4: Targeting

There is one main targeting option within Google Ads that you will want to pay attention to – location targeting. Location targeting allows you to target people in your specific city or geographic area. You can control this in your settings at the campaign level.

Step 5: Paying for Ads

How Do You Pay for Ads?

Google ads are bought and sold through an "auction" system, which means that there isn't a set price for an ad. Ad pricing is based on supply (how many people are searching for the keyword on Google) and demand (how many advertisers want to reach that audience), as well as how good the ad is.

- How much you are willing to pay
- How much your competition is paying
- How good your ad is (user value)

 Power Tip! *You can actually outrank your competition and pay less per click than they do. How? By having a higher-quality ad. High-quality ads have keywords in the ad that aligns with the content the user will find on the page. Your ads will have a higher quality score if users click on the ad and spend time on your site.*

Setting A Budget

Use the Google Keyword Planner to get an estimate of what you should expect to pay. You can set a daily budget or campaign end date to control your budget. Start small so you can learn what drives results and increase your budget as you grow.

 Power Tip: *When setting your budget, consider your estimated return on investment. How many new customers could this reasonably result in for your business, and what does that translate to in revenue dollars? This will help you set a reasonable budget.*

Step 6: Optimization

Once an ad starts to run the results are visible immediately. Unlike traditional advertising you don't have to wait until the end of a campaign to see what works. You can test, learn and optimize as you go.

- Test different ad copy
- Test different bidding choices

Build a testing plan upfront so you can see what really works for you and continue to improve your ROI (return on investment). To setup a testing plan, you will need to setup tracking through your Google Analytics and your Google Ads.

The "ART" of SEO

For SEO to be effective, it's important to focus on the three key elements of SEO, which we refer to as the "ART" of SEO. All three elements must be given significant attention for SEO to work.

Authority

The search engines will rank you higher for a keyword if you are an authority for that keyword. Build authority by gaining links to your website from other relevant websites.

Relevance

If you want to rank for a keyword, you must use relevant keyword phrases in your content. Build a content strategy that focuses on relevant content that supports your keywords.

Technical

To rank in search engines, the search engine spiders must be able to find and index your site, and understand what you are about. Build a technically healthy site by adhering to the standards and best practices of SEO.

Build Authority

Authority refers to how important the search engines think you are, and how much of an authority you are in your industry or for the keywords you wish to rank.

Follow this checklist to build authority:

- ☐ Analyze your link profile
    - ☐ Do you have quality inbound links?
    - ☐ Do you have a large number of low-quality links that are harming your ranking? If so, consider the link disavow tool.

- ☐ Analyze your competitors' link profiles
    - ☐ Are there common sites that are linking to your competitors?
    - ☐ How many quality links do your competitors have compared to you?

- ☐ Know how to identify good-quality link opportunities
    - ☐ Good links are from content that is relevant to your page, domain, conversation, or topic that you want it to link to.
    - ☐ Good links drive traffic.
    - ☐ Good links provide value to the user.

- Identify linkable assets.
  - What content do you already have that is interesting and other sites might want to link to?
- Identify link opportunities
  - Using your Link Marketing Checklist, explore the different ways to identify new opportunities.
  - Use a tool or spreadsheet to maintain an organized plan.
- Link outreach
  - Call vs. email if possible (more personable).
  - If you email, provide value for the linking site to link to you, keep it short, use correct grammar and spelling, include clear contact information, and one clear call to action in your request.

Build Relevance

Relevance refers to how relevant your site content is to the keywords you want to rank for.

Follow this checklist to build relevance:

- Choose keyword targets that you have the highest probability of ranking for, and are most likely to generate quality traffic and revenue.

- Create a content strategy that aligns with the keywords you want to rank for. Your strategy should align with your overall goal for what you want to achieve with your website.

- Identify a main focus keyword for each page of your site that you want to rank, as well as supporting keywords to help the search engines understand what you are about.

- Use your keywords throughout your page in the title tag, meta description tag, heading tags (h1, h2, etc.), first 200 words of the copy, throughout the copy on the page, in alt tags, and text links.

Build Technical Health

Having a technically healthy site is critical to the success of your SEO plan. Remember that the search engines must be able to read the code of your site to determine what keywords you should rank for.

Follow this checklist to build a technically healthy site:

- Use the Google SEO Starter Guide as a starting point to identify the best practices of SEO.

- Conduct a website audit to identify and prioritize tasks to make your site technically healthy.

☐ Check Google Search Console periodically to understand how Google views your site and identify any needed improvements.

Analyze and Measure

Analytics are critical to a successful SEO Plan. Track and measure your efforts so you know what is working.

Follow this checklist to analyze and measure SEO success for your site:

☐ Use Google Analytics to track vital information about how users find your site and where they go once they are on your website.

☐ Use Google Tag Manager for managing tags and tracking without editing the website code directly.

☐ Setup tracking for your KPIs (key performance indicators) which indicate whether or not you are achieving your goals.

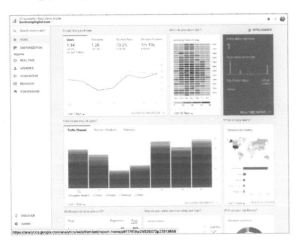 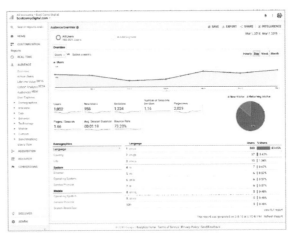

 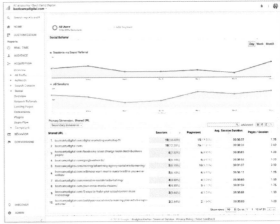

How Search Engines Work

Search engine spiders crawl the web and index everything they can find. Ranking factors influence what the user sees in the search results when they query a search engine. You improve your chances of ranking by building a technically healthy site that the search engines can find, using the right keywords in your content, and building relevant inbound links to your site.

Web Crawlers

Search engines use an automated program to send out search bots known as "crawlers" or "spiders" to crawl the web.

Analyze Site

Spiders evaluate and learn about a site by analyzing content, metadata and keywords, among other bits of data including links to other sites and pages.

Index

Spiders consolidate their findings from each page and build an index. The data is held in massive datacenters that have been constructed all over the world.

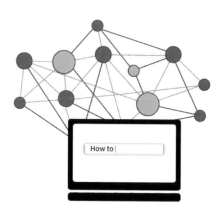

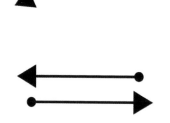

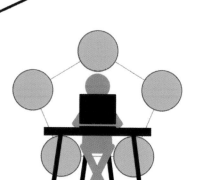

Search Engine

When a user types in a keyword query into a search engine, the search engine uses algorithms to scour its billions of indexes to pull out the most relevant results.

Search Engine Results Page (SERP)

The user is provided a ranked list of the pages the search engine has determined are the most relevant and most popular.

Paid vs. Organic

There are two types of search results – paid and organic. SEO focuses on practices that influence the organic search results.

Paid Search

- You pay the search engine to have your listing appear on the search results page (typically shows up at the top of the page).
- Indicated by an "Ad" icon or "Sponsored" text.
- On average, 20% of users click the paid search results.
- Google AdWords is the most widely used tool to create ads.

Organic Search

- A website's "natural" rankings.
- Rankings are determined by algorithms.
- SEO practices influence organic search results.
- On average, 80% of users click the organic search results.

Keywords

People enter keywords into a search engine to find answers and information. We call these searches "queries." If you want to be found for what your audience is searching for, you must use the same keywords they search for in your content. Your keywords are much more than just a list of your products and services.

Follow these guidelines for choosing the right keywords.

- ☐ List your products and services (i.e. gluten free cupcakes)
- ☐ List words that describe your industry or category (i.e. gluten free bakery)
- ☐ List the problems that your product or service solves (i.e. allergy friendly baked goods)
- ☐ List words and phrases that are related to your business (i.e. kids food allergies)
- ☐ List words and phrases that indicate an intent to buy (i.e. buy gluten free cupcakes online)

SEO Process and Workflow

A great way to develop an effective SEO strategy is to plan a workflow and process for the entire year. SEO is not something that can be completed all at once and is not something that is a single, fixed solution. Your SEO strategy will evolve as Google algorithms update, as your audience matures in their interests, and as you analyze new and existing competitors. Build a schedule to keep SEO integrated into your overall marketing plan and to keep SEO-related tasks an active part of your routine.

Use the checklist below as a guide as you develop your SEO strategy this year.

One-Time Setup	Daily / Weekly	Monthly	Quarterly / Yearly
□ Google Analytics and Google Tag Manager □ Google Search Console □ Yoast SEO □ Round 1 Technical SEO Cleanup □ Audits □ Links □ Content □ Technical □ Research □ Keywords □ Competition □ Industry □ Audience	□ Content Creation □ Link Marketing □ Social Media	□ Analytics □ Technical Health Check (GSC) □ Content Calendar	□ Audits □ Links □ Content □ Technical □ Research □ Keywords □ Competition □ Industry □ Audience

Top SEO Tools

- **Google PageSpeed Insights** – Analyze and optimize your website to make it faster. Use the PageSpeed tools to get your PageSpeed score and suggestions for how to improve the speed of your website.
  Check it out at https://developers.google.com/speed/

- **Google Trends** – See the latest keyword trends locally and globally.
  Use Google Trends to discover new keywords and spot trends in keyword usage over time. Compare the popularity of keywords and adjust your strategy when appropriate.
  Check it out at https://trends.google.com/trends/.

- **Google Keyword Planner** – Discover relevant keywords and monitor trends.
  Part of the Google Adwords platform, this free tool works to find keywords that are most relevant to your business. See how often keywords are searched and how their search volume changes over time.
  Check it out at http://adwords.google.com/KeywordPlanner.

- **Google Search Console** – Keep your site health in check.
  Curious how Google views your website? This tool provides insight into which keywords users are searching for when they land on your site. If this is your first time using this tool, you will need to verify ownership of your site, then allow Google time to gather data.
  Check it out at https://www.google.com/webmasters/tools/home.

- **SEM Rush** – Run a competitor analysis.
  Enter a competitor's web address and see the keywords that your competitors are ranking for. This tool will also show you other competitor websites to consider. You can register on the site for free and run up to ten requests. A paid subscription is also available. Check it out at https://www.semrush.com.

- **Yoast** – SEO plugin for WordPress sites.
  Use this tool to assist in creating title and meta descriptions based on your keyword. It also provides a page analysis, giving you suggestions for improving your content and SEO. Check it out at https://yoast.com/.

- **XENU's Link Sleuth** – Find broken links on websites.
  Keep your website usable and free from broken links or images. This tool is also useful for finding broken links on other sites, where there is an opportunity to offer a link to your own content in place of the outdated content. http://home.snafu.de/tilman/xenulink.html

- **Screaming Frog SEO Spider** – Evaluate and manage your on-page SEO.
  Generate a list of all your website pages and manage titles and meta tags, headings, word count and much more!
  https://www.screamingfrog.co.uk/seo-spider/

- **Answer The Public**– Uncover content ideas related to your keywords.
  Create content that answers the questions your audience is asking.
  https://answerthepublic.com/

SEO Keyword Research Exercise

Use this guide to build your keyword list and your SEO plan. This exercise will help you identify keyword opportunities to include in your content.

What are the words that people use to describe your product or service?

What are the words that people use to describe your industry/category?

What are the words that people use to look for your competition?
HINT: Use keyword research tools or look at metadata to research the words that your competitors are optimizing for – you may choose to compete directly or choose different keywords.

What are the words that people use to find information about the problem that you solve?

What are the words that people use to look for information related to your business?

What are the words that people use when they are looking to purchase your product or service?
HINT: These may be different than the products/services keywords. Think about how people search when they are ready to buy.

Is your business confined to any specific geography or sub category? (i.e. City/Town, Property Lawyer vs. Lawyer, etc.)

Are there any add-on words that are relevant for how people search for businesses in your industry?
For example:

Best (e.g. Best doctor in New York)
Cheapest (e.g. Cheapest dog day care)
Coupon
Deal
Top
Most popular
Fastest
Lowest Cost
For Small businesses/Big company/etc.
Specific verticals to target
Social Media for Real Estate Agents
Social Media for Lawyers
Social Media for Farmers
Other_____
Other_____

SEO Keyword Analysis

Follow this process to identify the best keyword targets to focus on. Good keywords are most likely to drive traffic that generates results and revenue.

1) **Go to the GOOGLE KEYWORD PLANNER https://adwords.google.com/KeywordPlanner**

2) **Input your search terms from the list you built above**

3) **Look at the additional recommended words from Google and add any relevant new words to your list**

 Power Tip: Use additional keyword research tips and tools for deeper keyword discovery.

4) **Go to www.google.com and type in allintitle:keyword phrase (replace keyword phrase with your keyword)**

5) **Record the number of returned search results (it appears right below the search box)**

6) **Note the intent of each keyword for the searcher. Is the term likely to generate revenue?**

7) **Prioritize the search terms based on the PRIORITY that they are for YOUR BUSINESS, the PROBABILITY that you can rank for them, and the LIKELIHOOD that they will drive revenue.**

A good search term has some search volume but low search results AND is likely to generate traffic that converts to a sale.

If your search terms are all returning too many results, consider adding the add-on words you created on page two to find more specific terms. For example, instead of "social media training," try "Cincinnati social media training," "best social media training" or "small business social media training."

Once you know the KEYWORDS (they may be individual words or phrases) that you want to optimize your site for, be sure to include the keywords on your website and social media profiles as appropriate. Include your keywords in any online content you create.

Keyword	Searches/Month	# of Search Results	Intent

Keyword Intent

Keywords can be different throughout the stages in the buying cycle. Choose keywords that are most likely to drive quality traffic. Then you can build a framework for creating relevant content that ranks well and drives traffic that converts.

Attract

The majority of searches online fall into this category where users are just beginning their journey on a path to purchase.

☐ Searchers are doing research, window shopping, looking for a solution but not sure what it is.

☐ Provide content that answers the questions they are asking at this stage such as "how to…" or "Why is…"

☐ Move users through the funnel via an email newsletter, blog subscription, social media follow, etc.

Power Tip: AnswerThePublic.com is a great site for discovering common questions around various topics.

Nurture

Nurture prospects and potential customers through the funnel and help them make a decision.

☐ Searchers are closer to purchase, but not sure who to buy from at this stage. They are familiar with the potential solutions to their problem. They are comparison shopping and researching their options.

☐ Provide content that helps educate the user and include keywords such as "product + reviews," "Best of…" or "Top 10…." Or choose keywords for specific products or the product category.

☐ Create content that helps in the decision-making process.

Convert

This is where an action takes place.

☐ Searchers are seriously considering the purchase and need a nudge to make the decision, or they are ready to buy.

☐ Provide content that helps the user who is ready to take action with keywords like "buy" or your brand name.

☐ Include clear call to action.

Retain/Grow

Don't stop at the conversion! It's easier to grow loyal customers than find new ones.

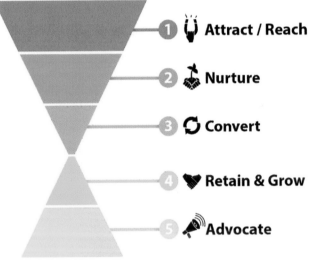

Marketing Funnel

1 👆 Attract / Reach
2 🐾 Nurture
3 🔁 Convert
4 💙 Retain & Grow
5 📢 Advocate

☐ Searchers are your new customers who want an easy onboarding process or to feel good about their purchase.

☐ Provide content that keeps them happy like support or special offers.

☐ Create training materials, help files, or manuals.

Advocacy

Positive reviews help you rank better. Protect your brand by building a positive reputation and trust with your audience.

☐ Your customers are your fans and want to share their experience.

☐ Provide content that helps build your reputation such as testimonials or success stories.

☐ Test your success with authentic video testimonials.

Local SEO

What is Local SEO?

SEO stands for Search Engine Optimization which gets your website ranked at the top of Google. Local SEO is about getting to the top of the maps results in Google when people are searching for your business or similar businesses nearby.

Why Local SEO is Important

Consumers are seeking out local businesses online now more than ever. Local SEO helps you reach local patients where they are searching. 56% of searches have local intent.

How to Dominate Local Search Results

To dominate local search, focus on these four tactics:

1 – Website Local SEO

SEO is a balance of getting links from other websites (Authority), building keyword rich content (Relevance), and building a site that the search engines can find and understand (Technical).

Follow these tips for adding a local component to each:

Authority

- ☐ Get links from local directories + websites
  - ☐ Search for "City + business directory" or "City + your industry directory" to find relevant directories. All sites are different, so look for a link or information on each site on how to add your listing.

 Power Tip: Do not pay for links! Unless there is a clear advertising opportunity and return on your investment, do not pay to be listed in a directory. In most cases, paid links do not help your SEO.

Relevance

- ☐ Use relevant keywords
  - ☐ Use geographic modifiers on your keywords: "Phoenix Eye Doctor"
  - ☐ In title and meta description on pages of your website

- In page content (headings & copy)
- Visible address and contact info on site (commonly placed in footer)

 Power Tip: Keywords are not limited to a list of your services. Consider keywords that signify buying or research intent: "find eyeglasses near me", "eye exam locations Chicago", "eye doctor Orlando", and "do I need glasses".

Technical

- Be sure that your website is optimized for search engines to find and understand your content without any problems. Technical SEO ensures that your website follows current search engine guidelines and can be ranked for the keywords you want to rank for. It's like building on a solid foundation. Your website developer should be able to help with this.

 Power Tip: Wordpress is the #1 platform that businesses use to power their websites, and it's SEO-friendly. Start a step ahead by building your website on Wordpress to avoid technical issues that could hurt your rankings.

2 – Local Directories & Websites

Maintain your listing in local directories and websites with accurate information about your location to ensure consistency in your listings. Consistency builds trust and gets higher rankings.

3 – Google My Business

The information in your listing appears in search results, but not just on Google products like Maps, Assistant, and Home. (View "How Many Places on the Internet Does Your GMB Listing Show Up?": http://bit.ly/gmblistings) Over 100,000 websites and apps have access to use the GMB data in their own content. It's an effective way to reach your patients where they are searching.

Check out the below tips & tricks for managing your Google My Business listing.

Claim + Verify

- Goal: 100% completion
- Claim: https://business.google.com/ and enter your business name and follow the prompts to claim an existing or create a new listing.
- Verify by phone or mail. If you verify by mail, be sure to notify whoever gets your mail each day to be on the lookout for something from Google.

Accurate Information

- Name
    - Full business name (CORRECT: Smith Dental)
    - No unnecessary info or extra keywords (WRONG: Dr. Bob the best dentist in Chicago)
    - Consistent with how you list your busines on other sites, and on your website

- □ Address
    - □ If multiple businesses are at teh same address, use Suite numbers to designate
    - □ If your business operates from a home address or you have a mobile business and no storefront, choose Yes under "I deliver goods and services to my customers at their location", then uncheck the box "I also serve customers at my business address" to hide your address from the public.
- □ Phone
    - □ Use local number (not toll free)
- □ Hours
    - □ Don't forget to update if you change hours

Category

- □ Use as few as possible
- □ Search + choose specific as possible

Description

- □ Overview of who you are/what you offer
- □ Include a call to action
  (i.e. "Schedule an appointment today!")
- □ Include relevant keywords
- □ 100-200 words

> Category
>
> Categories describe what your business is, not what it does or sells.
>
> Primary category
>
> Optometrist
>
> Additional categories
>
> ADD ANOTHER CATEGORY
>
> CANCEL   APPLY
>
> **Please note:** Edits may be reviewed for quality and can take up to 3 days to be published. Learn more

Photos (Images)

- □ Interior (builds credibility, shows that you are a real business)
- □ Exterior (helps customrs find your location and builds credibility as a real business)
- □ At work (your team in action, add personality)
- □ Team (profile photos)
- □ Identity (cover photo, profile photo, logo)

 Power Tip: If you are a solo practitioner within a practice, use a professional headshot for your logo. If you own a practice and have a logo, use the logo for your practice.

4 – Ratings & Reviews

Businesses with good reviews get more visibility and more customers. 93% of consumers say that positive reviews influence their purchase decisions.

- Build a Plan:
    - Who will respond + timeframe
    - Create resoponses in advance for anticipated positive and negative reviews

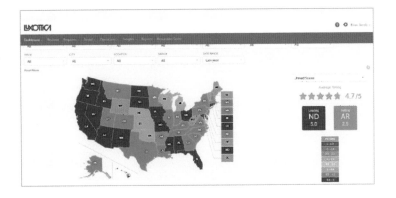

- Get Reviews
    - Ask! 70% of consumers will leave a review for a business when asked.
    - Create a link for customers to write reviews and share this link via email, on your website, no social media, etc. https://support.google.com/business/answer/7035772?hl=en

- Monitor + Respond
    - Respond to all reviews when able – remember this impacts your SEO and reputation!
    - At the very least, respond to all negative reviews

Why Does Website Speed Matter?

Site speed is growing in importance online as consumers become less patient and expect faster sites. Increased mobile traffic contributes to this trend as slower network speeds means sites need to load quickly.

- **Traffic** – Slow sites means less traffic as people leave your site instead of waiting for it to load.
- **User experience** – Users won't have a good experience with your site and are less likely to convert.
- **Search prominence** – Google de-prioritizes slow sites in search results.
- **Facebook traffic** – Facebook de-prioritizes content from slow loading sites in the newsfeed.

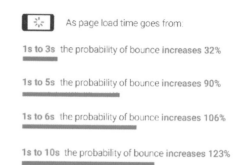

As page load time goes from:

1s to 3s the probability of bounce increases 32%

1s to 5s the probability of bounce increases 90%

1s to 6s the probability of bounce increases 106%

1s to 10s the probability of bounce increases 123%

How Can you Check your Website Speed?

There are a few tools that you can use to check your website speed.

- GTMetrix – www.gtmetrix.com – score and detailed breakdown of speed errors.
- Google Speed Test - https://developers.google.com/speed/pagespeed/insights/ - speed on mobile & desktop, score & issues.
- Google Mobile Speed Test - https://testmysite.thinkwithgoogle.com/ - mobile speed and any issues.

What is "good" Speed?

1) How fast is your site – Google suggests that you aim for under 3 seconds.
2) Are there errors preventing it from being faster – Regardless of your speed you can take action to fix these items to improve your site performance.

What Impacts Site Speed?

Site speed is generally a result of the following 3 elements. A report from GTMetrix or Google will provide you with details about which of these elements are causing your site to be slow.

1) Technical elements on the page – how code is organized and displayed and how the site is setup.
2) Content – content on the site and how it is presented and optimized (or not).
3) Hosting – the type of hosting you have and location.

How can you Fix your Speed?

Fixing site speed can be complex as it depends on the specific factors causing your site to be slow. The best approach is to run a report on GT Metrix and discuss with your web developer how to fix the issues that are impacting speed.

What Are My Objectives?

Why are you building or redesigning a website? (The wrong answer is "it's been a while since we redesigned" or "I don't like how it looks".) What you need to ask is, what do you want to accomplish with your website? (IE: increase traffic to site, increase leads or generate sales, increase blog subscribers).

 Power Tip: Tie your objective to measurable results. A "pretty" website is NOT a good objective. A website that sells more products IS a good objective.

Who is My Audience?

This may seem obvious, but consider this: the primary user may not be the purchaser. Therefore the purchaser might be interested in different information than the user. Think of what's important to the persona that you're actually selling to. How does your website serve your audience?

What Are We Currently Doing Wrong (or Right)?

Look at your **Google Analytics** to determine what pages are already getting a lot of traffic and/or conversions, or what pages aren't but should? Look at **Google Search Console** to determine what pages are already ranking well or not at all. What pages are most popular?

What is the Buying Cycle?

Determine the content you need to meet people at every stage of the purchase path. People visit your site multiple times before making a decision. 92% aren't there to "buy now". Identify what else they are there for and build content for that.

 Power Tip: Consider all stages of the buying cycle and how your content can help move your audience though the purchase path to a sale.

What Are Competitors Doing?

How can you position yourself better than the competition? Is there a need for content on a popular or trending topic that no one has covered yet? What is common among competitors that you should be doing? Or how are you different/better?

What is My Value Proposition?

What else are you selling other than your product or service? Is it security? Saving money? How does this make you the better choice for your audience than your competition?

Information Expected To Be on Your Site

These are the types of content that appear
on most business and professional websites.

Every website should have this information.

- ☐ Contact
- ☐ About
- ☐ Product/Service Overview
- ☐ Links to Social Media
- ☐ Reviews
- ☐ Call to Action

Home Page

Your home page is your first impression to most of your audience, and you only have a few seconds to get
their attention and make it clear what your website isabout. Make sure you home page:

- ☐ Has clear messaging so the user can figure out what you do.
- ☐ Has clear messaging so a user knows what your site is about within just a few seconds.
- ☐ Has clear navigation so the user can easily find their way around the site.

Common Website Design Practices

Consider these common website design practices when building your site:

- ☐ Logo in top left
- ☐ Contact in top right
- ☐ Main navigation across top
- ☐ Home page slider image
- ☐ Clear value proposition at top of home page
- ☐ Clear call to action at top of home page
- ☐ Site search feature
- ☐ Sign-up form for newsletter/blog in footer
- ☐ Social media icons in footer
- ☐ Mobile responsive design

What is Google My Business?

Google My Business is a free tool for businesses to manage their online listings, commonly referred to as Google Maps. The information in your listing appears in search results, but not just on Google products like Maps, Assistant, and Home. (View "How Many Places on the Internet Does Your GMB Listing Show Up?" http://bit.ly/gmblistings) Over 100,000 websites and apps have access to use the GMB data in their own content. It's an effective way to reach your customers where they are searching.

Why Google My Business is Important

Consumers are seeking out local businesses online now more than ever. 56% of searches have local intent. Google holds the market share for search, so it only makes sense that if you want to appear for localized searches, you will achieve the most reach through Google My Business. To dominate the Google Maps results, you need a Google My Business Listing and positive reviews.

Google My Business Setup

Claim + Verify

- ☐ Goal: 100% completion
- ☐ Claim: https://business.google.com/ and enter your business name and follow the prompts to claim your listing, if it exists, or create a new listing.
- ☐ Verify: by phone or mail. If you verify by mail, be sure to notify who picks up your mail to be on the lookout for mail from Google.

Accurate Information

- ☐ Name
  - ☐ Full business name
  - ☐ Consistent with how you list your business on other sites, and on your website
- ☐ Address
  - ☐ Google understands that multiple businesses may operate from the same address. No need to use suite numbers to designate.
  - ☐ If your business operates from a home address or you have a mobile business and no storefront, choose Yes under "I deliver goods and services to my customers at their location", then uncheck the box "I also serve customers at my business address" to hide your address from the public.

- ☐ Phone
  - ☐ Use local number (not toll free)
- ☐ Hours
  - ☐ Don't forget to update if you change hours

I deliver goods and services to my customers at their location — Important information

◉ Yes　○ No

My business delivers goods & services to customers within this area:

◉ Region, city or postal code　　　　　ADD

○ Within　0　　mi ⌄　of my business

☐ I also serve customers at my business address. (Your address will be hidden from the public if this box isn't checked.)

Category

- ☐ Use as few as possible
- ☐ Search + choose specific as possible

Category

Categories describe what your business is, not what it does or sells.

Primary category

Training Centre

Additional categories

ADD ANOTHER CATEGORY

　　　　　　　CANCEL　　APPLY

Please note: Edits may be reviewed for quality and can take up to 3 days to be published. Learn more

Business Description

- ☐ Overview of who you are and what you offer
- ☐ Include a call to action
- ☐ Include relevant keywords
- ☐ 100-200 words

Photos (Images)

- ☐ Interior (builds credibility, shows that you are a real business)
- ☐ Exterior (helps customers find your location and builds credibility as a real business)
- ☐ At work (your team in action, add personality)
- ☐ Team (profile photos)
- ☐ Identity (cover photo, profile photo, logo)
- ☐ Aim for at least 10 photos and add more as you have relevant photos to share

Ratings & Reviews

Businesses with good reviews get more visibility and more customers. 93% of consumers say that positive reviews influence their purchase decisions.

- ☐ Build a Plan:
  - ☐ Who will respond + timeframe
  - ☐ Create responses in advance for anticipated positive and negative reviews
- ☐ Get Reviews
  - ☐ Ask! 70% of consumers will leave a review for a business when asked.
  - ☐ Create a link for customers to write reviews and share this link via email, on your website, on social media, etc. https://support.google.com/business/answer/7035772?hl=en
  - ☐ Aim to have at least 10 reviews and build over time
- ☐ Monitor + Respond
  - ☐ Respond to all reviews when able – remember this impacts your SEO and reputation!
  - ☐ At the very least, respond to all negative reviews

Posts

Businesses can post timely information about events, products and services, news, and special offers in Google My Business for free. Posts appear on Maps results, desktop search results and in business listings, along with many other places throughout the web.

Grub Burger Bar
on Google

Looking for a great Valentines day deal? Look no further! We are celebrating February 11th-16th with our love filled...

6 days ago

Create A Post

- ☐ Minimum 1XMonth (recommended 3+/Month)
- ☐ **Anchor Post** - Set a post to display for the entire month. Use this post as a business's core competency.
- ☐ **Secondary Posts** - Set a post to display for the first half of the month and a post to display for the second half of the month. Use these posts to promote specials, events, and other unique content.
- ☐ Post Ideas
    - Core Message
    - Specials, Sales, Coupons
    - New Products and Services
    - Events
    - Social Media Campaigns
    - Contests
    - Introduce Team Members
    - Virtual Tour Integration
    - Charity and Community Action
    - Holiday messages

A positive user experience is critical for earning and retaining customers. Your website should include each of the following elements for a positive user experience:

Useful

- ☐ Original content
- ☐ Fulfills a need
- ☐ Provides value
- ☐ Can be non-practical (fun or aesthetic)

Usable

- ☐ Website is easy to use
- ☐ It is easy to complete a task

Findable

- ☐ Navigation makes important pages easily findable
- ☐ Site search allows users to search larger websites
- ☐ Site is optimized to rank in search (SEO)

Credible

- ☐ Clearly labeled navigation
- ☐ Visuals (colors + content) are professional and align with the overall brand tone
- ☐ No typos, broken links, or errors

Desirable

- ☐ Appeals to emotions
- ☐ Engaging

Accessible

- ☐ Works for all users
- ☐ Accessible to people with disabilities
- ☐ Works on all main browsers (Chrome, Firefox, Safari)
- ☐ Works on all devices (Mobile, Desktop, Tablet)

Valuable

- ☐ Website content adds value to the user by providing information that can't be found elsewhere

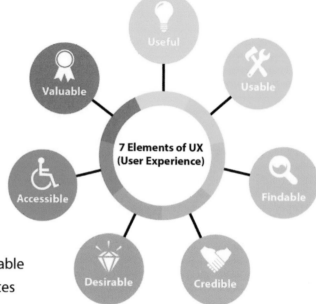

Why SEO?

Search engine optimization (SEO) is all about engineering your website so it ranks at the top of search engine results. As smart as the search engines are becoming, they still do not interpret website content the same way a human can. SEO is necessary to help the search engines understand what your website is about and the keywords it should be ranking for.

Website SEO Overview

When optimizing your website to rank in search engines, the critical first step is choosing the right keywords. The next step is to optimize your pages by incorporating your keywords into your website so the search engines can understand the topics your site is about and what you should be ranking for.

Step 1: Choose the Right Keywords

People enter keywords into a search engine to find answers and information. If you want to be found for what your audience is searching for, you must use the same keywords they search for in your content. Your keywords are much more than just a list of your services.

Follow these guidelines for choosing the right keywords.

- ☐ List your services (i.e. eye exams, annual eye exams)
- ☐ List words that describe your industry or category (i.e. eye care center, vision center, eye doctor, optometrist)
- ☐ List the problems that your product or service solves (i.e. blurred vision, how to get my child to wear their glasses)
- ☐ List words and phrases that are related to your business (i.e. does looking at a computer damage your eyes, computer vision syndrome, glasses vs. contacts)
- ☐ List words and phrases that indicate an intent to buy (i.e. buy contact lenses)

Step 2: Optimizing Your Website Pages

If you want to rank for a keyword, then it needs to appear on your website. Often, businesses assume that their human users will intuitively understand what their website is about, and this results in important keywords being left out of website content. However, search engines need clarity and context to understand what keywords you should rank for. Unfortunately, Google cannot read between the lines and assume what you are trying to say. Therefore, when optimizing your site, it's important that each page has a clear keyword focus.

- ☐ Your homepage should include your main target keywords which describe who you are and what you do.
- ☐ Build a separate page for each keyword theme that you wish to rank for.
    - ○ Main landing pages: eye doctor, eye exams, eye health, contact lenses, etc.
    - ○ Secondary/supporting pages: IE: blog posts about related topics or specialized topic areas of expertise "how to get your kids to wear glasses", "do computer screens damage vision", "how does diabetes affect your eyesight".

- ☐ I have chosen target keywords to use on the page. Target keywords are the keywords related to the main theme of each individual page.
- ☐ Each optimized page has one main theme or focus.
- ☐ My keyword is in the first 200 words of text on the page.
- ☐ I am using my main keywords throughout my writing.
- ☐ I am including related, or supporting, keywords to help clarify the meaning of my content. IE using "eye doctor" and "optometrist".
- ☐ My keyword is in the heading.
- ☐ My keyword is in the title tag.
- ☐ My keyword is in the meta description tag.
- ☐ My total number of words is similar to the total number of words on the top-ranking pages for my target keyword.

 Power Tip: *If you have a WordPress website, use a plugin like Yoast SEO that assists in creating title and meta descriptions based on your keyword, and provides a page analysis, giving you suggestions for improving your content and SEO.*

The best defense is a good offense. Having positive reviews is the best way to defend against negative reviews. Studies actually show that perfect ratings seem contrived, as 82% of consumers actually look for less-than-stellar feedback.

Why Are Reviews So Important?

Online buyers are skeptical, but word of mouth and opinions from other people are among the top purchase influencers.

Studies show that:

- 84% of people give online reviews the same consideration as a personal recommendation.
- 90% of consumers form an opinion about a business based on less than ten reviews.
- 74% of people trust a business more based on positive reviews.

When conducting an online search, business or product reviews typically show up directly in search results, along with the star ratings.

For many businesses, the business name + reviews is a common search term showing that people are actively looking for reviews.

4-Step Positive Review Strategy:

1. **Identify Review Site to Target**
   Start by identifying the sites where you want to get reviews. For most businesses this starts with:

   - Google
   - Facebook
   - Yelp
   - GlassDoor
   - Better Business Bureau
   - LinkedIn (personal)
   - Industry sites:
     - Trip Advisor, RateMyProfessor, etc

Start with the most important site for you to target first. Once you have built up a positive reputation on one site you can expand to the next.

If you aren't sure where to start, consider:

- Which review sites already show up in Google search results for your business?
- Which review sites show up in search results for your competitors?
- What industry sites do people visit?
- Which sites show up in searches for the category (e.g. Hotel in Amsterdam)?

2. Determine Ideal Number of Reviews

Look at how your competitors are displayed on the site as well as the characteristics of the review site itself.

- How many reviews do competitors have?
- How many reviews does it take to display a star rating?
- What is realistic for the size of your business?

3. Initial Ask of Reviews

Start by asking people who you know have had a good experience with you and are likely to give a good review. You'll want to have a base of positive reviews to start with.

- Ask them personally (mass messages are not great)
- Set a clear goal for yourself
  - Ask 3 people per week
- Build over time – some sites will think it is not natural if you suddenly go from 0 reviews to 40 in one week and could suspend your account
- Tell them EXACTLY where to write the review and how
- Make your request personal and authentic

AVOID THE TEMPTATION TO LEAVE FAKE REVIEWS! Most networks can spot these and they won't be published or may even lead to your account being blocked. Some businesses have also landed in legal trouble for leaving fake reviews.

Ask happy customers – this is a better strategy in the long run.

4. Operationalize Reviews

Build a strategy for your business to ask for reviews on a regular basis. Companies that have the best reviews often have a specific strategy to ask customers to leave them. There are four steps to operationalizing your review process:

a) Touchpoint analysis - What are all of the touchpoints you have with a customer when they could leave a review.

b) Optimal experience – Determine when in your experience with a customer is the ideal time to ask. You may have more than one. Is it when they receive your product in the mail? A few weeks later? After they attend your class?

c) Segment the ask – Consider segmenting the ask so that you are only asking people who you KNOW have had a good experience.

> For example, you can send an email after purchase with two links – if they had a good experience or have ways for you to improve. If they have ways to improve send them to a form on your website. If they had a great experience send them to a review site.

d) Get Alerts – Get alerts for when reviews are left for the most common websites. This will allow you to know if your ask strategy is working and if there are any reviews that you should pay attention to.

WARNING: Most websites have terms of service that prohibit businesses from incentivizing reviews. This means that you typically can't offer a discount or other incentive for a positive review.

 Power Tip: Get more Google Reviews by creating a link for users to leave a review easily in one click. Follow Google's step-by-step process here: http://bit.ly/create-review-link Or use this free tool to generate your link: https://whitespark.ca/google-review-link-generator/

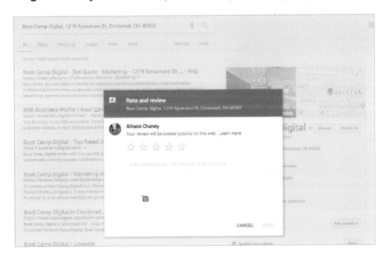

Avoiding Bad Reviews

The best approach where possible is to avoid bad reviews altogether. The following steps will help you to avoid them. Many people leave bad reviews simply because they don't feel heard or validated by the company. You can't win everyone over, but you can reduce bad reviews when you have the opportunity:

1. Open up Communication Channels

Most people don't leave a bad review unless they have already contacted the company. If the company is difficult to reach or not responsive they resort to a review. Allow people to contact you in as many different ways as possible.

2. Respond Quickly

Even if you don't have an answer right away, respond immediately (personally – not through an automated message) so people know you are looking into it. Giving people time to sit and stew feeling ignored is a good way to get poor reviews.

3. Be Nice + Build Connections

Customer service studies show that we are less likely to complain about people we like. Friendly doctors are sued less often. One of the keys to people liking you is to build rapport based on common interests. Apple has great customer service and their phone support is trained to find natural connection points (I see you are from Ohio – I used to live there!) to build a connection in the first few minutes of the call.

4. Empower Employees

Mistakes will be made – empower your employees to make things right to minimize the probability that a customer leaves a bad review. Sometimes small gestures can go a long way.

5. Set Expectations + Communicate with Customers

Most people are reasonable (not all). If you are having an issue that you think could result in a negative experience set expectations and acknowledge it.

Imagine if you are seated at a restaurant and the server immediately informs you "We had a big group just come in, so I think the kitchen may be slow and it could take about 30 minutes for your order to be ready. I'll be sure to keep your drinks topped up while you wait." This simple warning changes the experience from bad – waiting too long for food – to good – attentive drink refills.

Steps For Dealing With Negative Reviews:

No matter how great your business is, negative reviews will probably happen. Here are some tips to deal with them.

1. **Keep it professional** – While it's tempting to defend yourself or recount the details of the customer's behavior during the experience in question, it's rarely a good look. No one ever wins when debating online. Keep your answer courteous and polite.

2. **Don't get defensive** – While you may be right, defending your business at all costs is rarely a good strategy. Step back, try to see the situation from the customer point of view, and cool off before responding.

3. **Respond quickly** – Even if you are just looking in to it, the longer people wait for an answer the more upset they get. While you may be working a solution or investigating let the user know – otherwise they may feel ignored and continue to escalate.

4. **Respond Personally** – Canned responses can be infuriating and make the commenter or reviewer feel ignored. Make your response personal so that it is clear that you actually care.

5. **Directly Address the Issue** – Don't dance around the issue or use generalities. Address it as directly and specifically as possible. This shows that you care.

6. **Empathize without admitting fault** – Show empathy for the other persons situation. You'd be frustrated too if you waited on hold for two hours, got the wrong order, found an error with a consultant report or fill in the blank. You can empathize without admitting fault so the person feels heard.

7. **Always offer a public response in the same channel** – When you can, offer a public response in the same channel. This allows OTHER PEOPLE to see that you care and are responsive. Even if you can't win over the reviewer, your customers will see the review and observe how you handled it. If you got a comment on Facebook, respond on Facebook – don't try to push the dialogue to your website.

8. **Do your best to take it off-line** – Offer to call the reviewer, ask the reviewer to call you, or suggest they stop in to talk to a manager. You don't want endless back and forth adding drama. Words on a screen are subject to dramatic interpretation. Real people having a real conversation resolve problems. Plus, by publicly offering to connect with the reviewer you convey that you're interested in hearing about their experience and you're making yourself available to them. If they choose not to engage further with you, that's on them.

9. **Have a few templates ready to deploy** – You can't please everyone. Say it aloud with me. "I can't please everyone." There will be reviews that are worthy of an investigation and those that aren't. Start with these three responses and customize them as necessary.
   - "Thank you for letting us know about your experience. We'll look into it."
   - "Thank you for sharing thoughts about your visit. We strive to satisfy our customers. Please call us or come in to speak with a manager so we can learn more."
   - "Thank you for your thoughtful feedback. Sometimes criticism of our services is hard to hear, but it often leads to positive change. We appreciate your willingness to give us that opportunity to improve."

10. **When you don't have anything nice to say, don't say anything at all** – Your mom wasn't wrong. When you've attempted to reach out to the reviewer, yet they continue to berate you online, don't engage. Trust us on this – going toe-to-toe in the virtual world with a reviewer who is intent on making you look bad is NEVER a good idea. You'll come off as defensive, immature, and easily provoked, even if none of those characterizations are accurate. A virtual argument will speaker louder than the most glowing of reviews. Disengage totally.

11. **Know if Review Sites Can be Updated** – Some sites can be updated after the initial review. If you have a bad review but you make it right, consider asking the person to update their review if you are able to turn things around.

What is Email Marketing?

Email is one of the most effective forms of marketing, and businesses who are doing it right are getting big results.

Why is Email Marketing Important?

With 95% of online consumers using email, it is an extremely effective way to reach your audience, especially because 61% of them actually like to receive weekly promotional emails. People prefer to be contacted by email and it is one of the top marketing tools used by small businesses.

Not only is it widely used, but it's effective and relatively easy to implement vs. other marketing tactics. The ROI of an email is $40 for every $1 spent which is significantly greater than other forms of digital marketing. And emails have a greater click through rate than ads.

How to Get Results from Email Marketing

The key to success with email marketing is to approach it strategically. Before you begin your campaign, identify your main objective. Is the purpose of your email to sell products, generate leads, drive website traffic or something else? When building your list, creating content that interests the audience, and creating a call to action, you will see greater results when you tie these activities into your overall business objective. Integrate your email campaigns with your other marketing efforts to maximize your results.

How to Get Started with Email Marketing

There are 3 basic steps to building an effective email marketing campaign. To get started, you need to focus on:

1. Get email addresses
2. Get them to open the email
3. Get them to take action

Get Email Addresses

There are three ways you can collect email addresses:

- Buy a list (not recommended as these are often very low quality)
- Online – Consider online touchpoints where you can collect an email address:
  - Website: collect email addresses through a contact form, newsletter sign up form etc.
  - Email: Include a link to subscribe to your newsletter or blog. (Keep in mind the list you are emailing to. You wouldn't want to invite users to subscribe if they are already subscribers. This works best for new customers or initial emails with a new prospect.)

- o Email: Include a "forward to a friend" link in your emails, to encourage existing subscribers to share with a friend who may also want to join the list.
- o Social Media: Run Facebook ads that capture their name and email, add a sign up form to your Facebook page, or link to your list sign up page on your website in a social media post.
- Offline - Consider offline touchpoints where you have an opportunity to collect an email address:
  - o Tradeshow: get a list of attendees, collect business cards
  - o In store: Point-Of-Sale (POS) System, loyalty program, sign up sheet at register, collect business cards
  - o Networking events: collect business cards

Get Them to Open Emails

Getting people to open your emails is all about the subject line. Craft a catchy subject line that gets their attention, and clearly explains exactly what they should expect when they open the email.

Get Them to Take Action

Once you've got them to open your email, now it's time to get them to take action. When crafting your emails, be sure to keep your business objective in mind and identify the call to action that best helps you reach that objective. Then include a clear call to action in every email.

Analyze + Optimize

Use analytics to gain insights about your email marketing campaigns and use what you learn to optimize your efforts. Most email marketing programs have analytics built in, so identify where these are in your dashboard, and track the following metrics:

- CTR (click through rate)
- Conversion Rate
- Bounce Rate
- List Growth Rate
- Share/Forward Rate
- Overall ROI

When analyzing your metrics, it's important to understand what "good" looks like. This is best done by understanding industry benchmarks as well as benchmarking your own data. As you test different variants in your emails, analyze how this impacts your metrics to determine which types of emails and which variants perform best. There are two places where you will find the metrics related to your email marketing campaigns:

- Google Analytics
- Email Marketing Software

Email Strategy

Strategic thinking is the key to success with your email marketing campaigns. Email marketing can be effective at any stage of the marketing funnel. Use this guide to help build email content that aligns with your strategy.

Attract/Reach
- ✓ Educate them about your business/brand
- ✓ Welcome them to your community, group, etc.

Nurture
- ✓ Personalize your email content for your audience
- ✓ Build know, like + trust
- ✓ Help them make a decision by providing valuable information

Convert
- ✓ Have a clear call to action
- ✓ Show clear benefit to reader – what's in it for them if they complete the action?

Retain & Grow
- ✓ Build loyalty by making them feel special/exclusive
- ✓ Be useful and relevant and create content that is a good fit for existing customers

Advocate
- ✓ Encourage shares with friends
- ✓ Encourage positive reviews

Create A Clear Value Proposition

When asking people to join an email list, make sure you offer a compelling reason for them to join the list. Here are some reasons that might encourage someone to share their email address:
- ✓ Get coupons
- ✓ Early access to a sale/new product
- ✓ Free resources
- ✓ Free anything
- ✓ Contest entry
- ✓ Birthday club
- ✓ Sneak peek at content
- ✓ Solve a specific problem for them

Create A Great Subject Line

Your subject line needs to get their attention and make them want to open the email. This step is critical in the success of your campaigns. If they don't open the email, you've lost them. Here are some tips for creating a great subject line:

✓ Short (<30 characters perform best)
✓ Grabs attention
✓ Personalized ("Mary, check out these hand-picked looks!")
✓ Avoid spammy words and characters like "free", "act now", and "$$$"
✓ Don't mislead
✓ Consider using emojis

Create A Clear Call-To-Action

Once they open your email, it should be clear what action you want them to take. An email without a clear call to action is basically pointless, and you risk losing your subscribers. Follow these tips for creating a clear call to action that aligns with your overall business objectives:

✓ Placement = in the top 3rd of the email
✓ Short = 2-5 words
✓ Color = align with brand logo OR bright colors (A/B Test to see what works best)
✓ Urgency = use restrictions and action phrases: "download now", "limited time"
✓ One clear purpose = don't confuse with multiple choices
✓ Clear value proposition = What will I get if I click?

Measure + Analyze Results

When you know what "good" looks like you can identify the types of emails and variants that get the best results. Use this cheat-sheet to identify the benchmarks you should be setting and how to measure your success against what "good" looks like.

✓ CTR (click through rate)
  o Overall avg: 1-10%
  o Varies by industry/study
✓ Conversion Rate (the rate of people completing an action within the email)
  o Overall avg: 1-5%
  o Varies based on the purpose of the email
✓ Bounce Rate
  o Aim for < 2%
  o Overall avg: 9.60%
  o > 5 – 10% indicates you have a potential issue with the quality of your list
✓ List Growth Rate
  o Benchmark against your own data
  o Measure as a result of marketing efforts
  o Also pay attention to unsubscribes/bounces as they affect list size
✓ Share/Forward Rate
  o This is one type of conversion you might track – the action you measure is the share / forward
  o Connects to list growth rate – does asking people to share/forward affect list growth?
✓ Overall ROI
  o Overall avg: 122%
  o Overall avg: $40 for every $1 spent
  o Performs better than social and paid search ads

What is Inbound Marketing?

Inbound marketing is a technique for drawing customer to products and services through online content marketing, social media marketing, search engine optimization, and branding. It is a strategy that uses "pull marketing" to attract clients to you. It is designed to bring qualified leads to your business and convert them over time.

Rather than pushing your message at people – through outbound sales teams or advertising – you create content and employ a digital strategy that attracts prospects to you.

HubSpot has distilled the process of inbound marketing down to Attract, Engage, and Delight.

The 3 Stages of Inbound Marketing

1) **Attract**
   Attract is what draws prospects in to your business, and this could be paid or organic. A strong attract strategy brings the highest qualified leads to you.

2) **Engage**
   The engage tools create a relationship by getting the right message to the right person at the right time. The main objective of engage is to draw them in to engage so you can capture their information and continue to communicate with them.

3) **Delight**
   Finally, in the delight stage the emphasis is on automation and sales teams to deliver the right information to inspire them to actually do business with you.

Attract Tools	**Engage Tools**	**Delight Tools**
Ads	Lead Flows	Smart Content
Video	Email Marketing	Email Marketing
Blogging	Lead Management	Conversations Inbox
Social Media	Conversational Bots	Attribution Reporting
Content Strategy	Marketing Automation	Marketing Automation

 Power Tip: Before investing in CRM or inbound marketing software nail some of the basic elements required for success. Build a solid content and lead generation strategy prior to tackling the post-lead conversion process.

Should I Use Chatbots?

If you are considering using Chatbots, start by thinking about how the Chatbot will solve a problem for your customer or target audience. Be sure to also consider the business benefit of your Chatbot so that you know that you have a strong value proposition for your organization.

Will your Chatbot have a clear customer benefit? Ask Yourself:

- ☐ Is there and indication that people want this? Does my audience already ask for this on Messenger or other platforms?
- ☐ What value is in it for my audience?
- ☐ What will my audience get out of a Chatbot?
- ☐ Will a Chatbot solve a problem that exists?
- ☐ How does having a Chatbot compare with how we currently solve the problem?
- ☐ Will a Chatbot provide a better experience vs. the current experience?
- ☐ How will people discover the Chatbot?

Will your Chatbot have a clear business benefit? Ask Yourself:

- ☐ What business metrics matter to me?
- ☐ Do my business metrics match a Chatbot use case?
- ☐ What does success look like?
- ☐ What KPIs will I measure?
- ☐ What are my targets or benchmarks?

Power Tip: Before jumping in to Chatbots, consider the complexity of the bot you want to create and be realistic about the costs.

How Much Do Chatbots Cost?

When evaluating the costs of the Chatbot, be sure to consider ALL of these factors:

Setup Costs

- ☐ Consumer journey mapping
- ☐ Technology
- ☐ Mapping paths for questions, answers, and interactions
- ☐ Creating/testing/optimizing AI (Artificial Intelligence)
- ☐ User-testing
- ☐ Internal time/resources

Launch Costs

- ☐ Monitoring live launch
- ☐ Initial promotion

Promotion Costs

- ☐ Media costs
- ☐ PR
- ☐ Ongoing promotion

Running Costs

- ☐ Technology costs
- ☐ Time to manage
- ☐ Updates
- ☐ Cost to promote and drive traffic

Optimization Costs

- ☐ Evaluate & improve customer experience

Measurement

Measuring the results of your digital marketing efforts and adapting your strategy based on real data will set you apart from your competition. Know what to measure and where to focus your efforts for maximum success.

Resources Included in this Section:

Measurement and analytics are the best way to make sure that your digital marketing is performing and to grow your results. More time in analytics helps you understand if your efforts are paying off and where you can improve.

To make the most out of this section, consider the following tips:

✓ **Tip 1.** Measure what matters and focus on impact.

✓ **Tip 2.** Use analytics to diagnose performance issues and take action.

✓ **Tip 3.** It isn't what you **can do** it is what you **should do**. Prioritize!!!!!

✓ **Tip 4.** Create an execution plan that focuses your efforts on your priorities.

Set KPIs

A KPI is a Key Performance Indicator. It indicates whether or not you are achieving your goals.

When choosing KPIs consider:

- ☐ Quality + Quantity metrics
- ☐ Primary + Seconday metrics (limited primary KPIs)
- ☐ Link to your business or marketing objectives

Establish Benchmarks

Establish benchmarks for your digital marketing so that you have a goal in mind for each KPI. The benchmark should be established in relation to your investment.

Improvement

- ☐ Look for improvement over time
- ☐ This is the most important metric as every business situation is unique
- ☐ Focus on this ahead of industry benchmarks – this is really all that you can control

Averages

- ☐ Industry standards

WATCHOUT! These are averages and may not be representative of your industry or approach.

- ☐ Internal Benchmarks – other brands/businesses
- ☐ External Benchmarks – agency partners

WATCHOUT! Beware of comparing to competitors – you don't know what they invest to get results.

Plan

- ☐ Realistic based on your plan + investment

Be Realistic

- ☐ The digital landscape is always changing and your results may change over time
- ☐ Use measurement to improve over time
- ☐ Be aware of industry news that can impact results

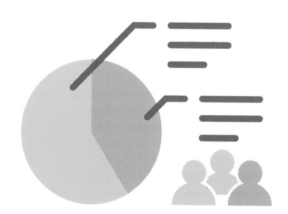

What is a KPI?

A KPI is a Key Performance Indicator – it is a metric that indicates whether or not your marketing efforts are achieving the desired business results. In marketing it is usually difficult and expensive to trace all activities back to sales (or the business goal you want to achieve). Instead, we rely on KPIs that allow us to measure the results of our marketing efforts and determine if they are working.

The idea is if I can't directly measure sales or new clients I want to track the things that suggest that I am getting sales or new clients. *For example, people in my target audience reading my blog and signing up for email indicates that I am driving interested people to my site which should lead to sales and clients over time.*

KPI = Key Performance Indicator
- Select few metrics that indicate success

Metrics/Measurement = Analysis + Insights
- Give us additional data, insights and optimization information

What makes a good KPI?

A strong KPI should:
- ☐ Be specific to your success
- ☐ Measurable
- ☐ Link to business objectives
- ☐ Focus on quality and quantity
- ☐ Incorporate costs of efficiency

The 3 Types of KPIs You Need

To really understand if your marketing is effective you'll want to be sure that your KPIs measure quantity, quality and cost. This gives you a full picture of your performance.

Quantity – How much am I getting?
- The amount of the result that you are generating
- EG: Traffic, traffic growth, clicks, reach, impressions

Quality – How good is what I'm getting?
- The effectiveness of the result or the quality of the result
- EG: Conversions, time on site, awareness growth

Cost – How cost effective is it?
- The cost per result or per quality to determine cost effectiveness
  - o Based on metrics/KPIs that matter for your business

What is a Benchmark?

A benchmark is a way to understand if your digital marketing is performing well relative to a set standard or benchmark. For example, you may have an open rate on your email of 10% - is this good? Should you be satisfied? What does good look like in digital marketing?

Benchmarking answers this question. It tells us if we are hitting an objective standard with our results. You may use a benchmark to evaluate your KPI performance or for other metrics that you evaluate.

KPI = Key Performance Indicator
- Select few metrics that indicate success

Metrics/Measurement = Analysis + Insights
- Give us additional data, insights and optimization information

Benchmark = Is our KPI or Measurement Acceptable?
- Provides context to the numbers and allows us to evaluate success

Setting a Strong Benchmark - IAP

While it can be tempting to set a benchmark based only on industry averages (for example aiming for a click-through-rate that matches industry standards) it is important to keep in mind that based on your unique business, marketing objectives and investment you may see valid differences.

- **I**mprovement
    - Look for improvement over time
- **A**verages
    - Industry standards
        - WATCHOUT: These are averages and may not be representative of your industry or approach.
    - Internal Benchmarks - other brands/businesses
    - External Benchmarks – agency partners
- **P**lan
    - Realistic based on your plan + investment

What Makes a Good Benchmark?
- ☐ Realistic
- ☐ Improvement vs. history
- ☐ Represents real success
- ☐ Linked to your investment

Google Analytics

The amount of data available to us in Google Analytics alone can be overwhelming. It's easy to be distracted by data that is easy to find but doesn't really tell us anything. The real value in data is the insights and actionable next steps that we can draw from it.

Success happens when we focus on measuring only what is important to driving your goals.

Use this checklist as a framework for what to look at every time you log in to Google Analytics. This list includes certain metrics that everyone should check as well as metrics that tie back to your specific goals. Think of the questions you want to answer, and the metrics that will best answer them.

Metrics That Matter in Google Anaytics:

- ☐ Total traffic
- ☐ Traffic sources (which are most effective at driving quality traffic/conversions?)
- ☐ New vs. Returning (are we filling the funnel?)
- ☐ Goals/Events (trackable actions taken on site)
- ☐ Mobile vs. Desktop (how did campaign perform, where to put more money)
- ☐ What sources drove best conversions and conversion rate?

Follow this method for analyzing data to get valuable insights.

Data Insights: 3W Method

- ☐ **What?** – What does the data tell me?
- ☐ **So What?** – Why is it happening? What does it mean to me?
- ☐ **Now What?** – What should I do about it? What will I change or do differently?

Google Analytics

What is Google Analytics?

Google Analytics is a free web analytics service (with paid options available for sites with significant traffic) offered by Google that tracks and reports website traffic.

 Power Tip: For most businesses, the free version of Google Analytics is the best option!

Why Google Analytics?

Digital analytics is important because people purchase goods as part of a process. There are multiple touch points and different actions that users take throughout this process. Digital analytics allows us to measure many aspects of the paths our users take in doing business with us and understand what online behavior led to their purchases. We can use this data to make smart decisions about how to reach new and existing customers. Google Analytics is the most widely used analytics platform and offers a cost-effective solution for businesses.

Creating a Google Analytics Account

Creating a Google Analytics account requires setup on the Google Analytics website which will generate a tracking code. This tracking code should be placed on every page of your website.

 Power Tip: Use the Gmail account you use for business activities to manage your Google Analytics account so you'll only need to stay logged in to one account. If you don't have a Gmail account for work, it's free and easy to create one and connect it to your work email.

Google Analytics Data

Reports in Google Analytics include dimensions and metrics. Dimensions are the things we want to measure (source of traffic, time on site, bounce rate, etc.) and the metrics are the data for the dimensions.

Google Tag Manager

What is Google Tag Manager?

Google Tag Manager is a tag management system created by Google to manage JavaScript and HTML tags used for tracking and analytics on websites.

When Should I Use Google Tag Manager?

If you are not a coding expert, or you have a lot of tagging to add and manage on your website, GTM might be right for you. It allows you to manage tagging and tracking of your website without needing to involve a developer every time.

Creating a Google Tag Manager Account

Creating a Google Tag Manager account requires setup on the Google Tag Manager website which will generate a tracking code. Follow the instructions on the GTM site once you've setup your account for adding the tracking code to your site. Then, you will use GTM to manage tagging of the actions you wish to track on your website.

What Can I Track with Google Tag Manager?

GTM allows you to setup tagging for tracking almost anything on your site. Here are a few common ways businesses are using GTM to manage tagging on their website:

- ☐ Form tracking
- ☐ PDF downloads
- ☐ External link clicks
- ☐ Adding tracking pixels to website for other services such as Facebook

Evaluate Success

When you evaluate your website analytics, you should focus on three things:

- ☐ Quantity
- ☐ Quality
- ☐ Cost

While an increase in traffic is usually good, it's also important to evaluate the quality of that traffic and what it cost you to acquire the traffic. This method for analysis is the foundation for gaining successful insights from your data to make smart marketing decisions.

What is ROI?

ROI stands for Return on Investment. ROI is calculated to understand if financial investments are paying out. While ROI seems simple (and it is) accurately calculating it is challenging, as we often don't know specifically the full return that our marketing efforts generate.

$$\frac{Return - Investment}{Investment}$$

Prior to embarking in ROI efforts, it is important to think about WHY you are calculating ROI. There are 2 main reasons:

1) Is this a profitable investment?
   - Focus on known data + reasonable assumptions to validate
   - Goal isn't to generate an accurate ROI number, but one that is directionally correct
   - May be other methods to achieve this

2) How does this compare to other uses of my funds?
   - Focus on consistency of methodology and assumptions across marketing efforts being measured
   - Very difficult to achieve

Calculating ROI: Return

Determining the return from marketing investments can be a challenge. Most marketing (traditional and digital) doesn't create an immediate action, and we know that many marketing efforts generate a benefit that is realized over time.

Often times marketing efforts aimed at "top of funnel" like awareness or interest are difficult to attribute specific sales to. Consider 3 things in determining your return:

- Directly attributable sales
- Indirect sales
- Additional benefits

1 Awareness
2 Interest
3 Desire
4 Action
5 Retention
6 Advocacy

For example, if you consider the value of a coupon, you have the direct benefit of sales from those who redeem the coupon (less those who would have purchased it anyways) + the media benefit from those who see the coupon and eventually buy, even without redeeming.

Also note, that in order to accurately calculate return you want to focus on the lifetime value of a new customer, not a single purchase. The "return" in ROI should be your profit for a lifetime customer, not sales.

Calculating ROI: Investment

When calculating the investment many businesses make the mistake of only incorporating initial costs to execute. In the ROI calculation you should include:

- Setup costs
- Indirect costs
- Media/promotion costs
- Run/maintenance/going costs
- Time/energy/internal people

Alternatives to ROI to Justify Investment

Calculating ROI can be very challenging, and it is important to keep in mind the *reason* for calculating ROI – to understand if we are making wise investments.

There are other ways to calculate this:

- **Backwards Math** – What do we need for this to be ROI positive? Does that seem reasonable?
  - If we spend $100K/year on social media, we need to gain or retain 10 new customers/year.

- **Back of Envelope Math** – What do we expect this to do? Does that generate positive ROI?
  - We assume that our "refer a friend" campaign will generate 5,000 new customers based on previous performance.

- **Translate KPIs to Sales** – Use reasonable assumptions to translate your KPIs to sales.
  - If we reach 100 people, let's assume we converted 1 of them. If we get 50 website visitors, we assume 1 becomes a lead.

Things to Consider

Profit Not Sales: Remember, when using any ROI or other approaches to calculate your return, look at the **lifetime profit** of a new customer – not sales and not a single purchase (unless you don't typically have repeat purchases).

Avoid the Trap: Try to avoid the measurement trap where you spend lots of time trying to get an accurate calculation for something that is based on many assumptions. Think about what you need to make a decision, and invest an appropriate amount of time.

Consider KPIs as an Alternative: Sometimes ROI is challenging (or impossible) to measure. For this reason, we often use KPIs to judge the value of our marketing investments. See the KPI Quick-Start for more details.

Where to Play

When choosing which social networks to participate in, remember that it is better to do a few things well vs. many things "ok". Choose to spend your time where you can get the best impact instead of trying to do everything.

Choose where to play based on these four things:

People
- ☐ Is your audience there?
- ☐ Are other businesses effectively reaching the target audience in this platform?

Network
- ☐ How does the network let businesses participate?
- ☐ How do people use the network and are they open to your message?

Return
- ☐ Estimated impact/business result?
    - ☐ Consider the probability of achieving your business/marketing goals
    - ☐ What does the best-case scenario look like?
    - ☐ What does expected-performance look like?
- ☐ What is the estimated annual impact?
    - ☐ Based on metrics/KPIs that matter for your business

Investment
- ☐ What is the estimated cost/time/effort to succeed?
- ☐ Consider time, tools, growing your following, etc.

Putting it Together

After conducting the above analysis, consider if you are likely to generate a positive ROI (Return on Investment) from your efforts.

Investment/Impact Priorities

Plot your investment options on the chart here. You can use this to evaluate the social networks that are most likely to grow your business and compare the relative investment/impact of each option.

This framework can also be used for any social media or digital marketing investment.

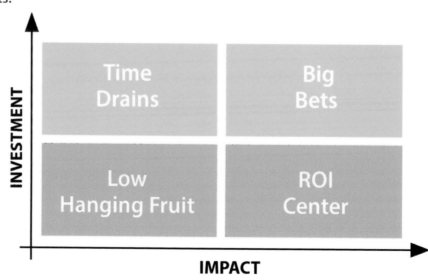

Hero / Hub / Hygiene Check

It is also helpful to evaluate where a social media activity lies in the HHH model.

Depending on the maturity level of your business, you should focus on Hygiene first, then Hub and eventually Hero or innovation.

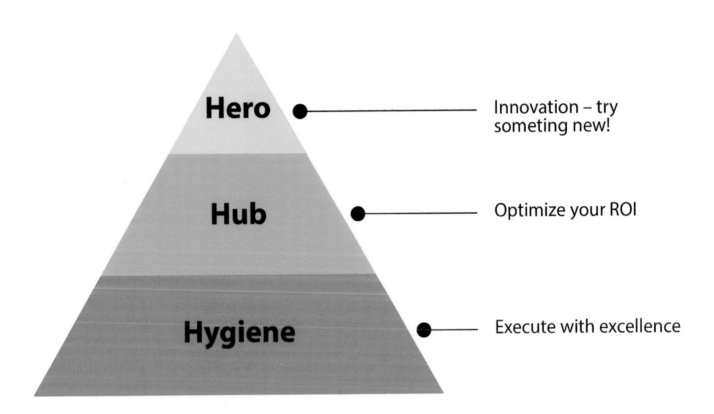

Don't be distracted by unproven networks and tools that can become time drains. These are the innovations that you should strategically limit to maintain your focus.

My primary goal for using digital marketing is:

_____

The digital strategies I will use to achieve this goal are:

1. _____

2. _____

3. _____

The people I am trying to reach are:

_____

Therefore, I am going to implement the following digital marketing tactics:

Immediately

Short-term (next 3 months)

Medium-term (3 – 6 months)

Long Term (6 months+)

HERO
Innovate

HUB
Optimize

HYGIENE
Execute with excellence

BOOT ★ CAMP
DIGITAL

Want to take your social media and digital marketing skills to the next level? Go to www.BootCampDigital.com to see how we can help you succeed.

What We Offer at Boot Camp Digital:

- Online training courses from Beginner to Advanced
- Industry-recognized Certifications in Social Media, Digital Marketing, Content, SEO, and more
- Live workshops around the U.S.
- Customized corporate team training
- Digital Marketing and Social Media consulting
- 1:1 Coaching and Strategic Planning

Connect with Us Online:

 bootcampdigital

 @bootcampdigital

 @bootcampdigital

 Boot Camp Digital

Contact us for speaking, training, consulting, seminar or workshop opportunities at: **info@bootcampdigital.com** or call us at **513-223-3878**.

Krista Neher is the CEO of Boot Camp Digital, a bestselling author of six books, international speaker and recognized digital marketing expert with over 15 years of experience in this ever-changing industry.

She has worked with leading companies like Google, P&G, General Mills, Nike, GE, The United States Senate, Prudential, Remax and more. She has also been a featured expert in the Wall Street Journal, The New York Times, CNN, Associated Press, Wired Magazine and CBS News.

Krista is passionate about social media and created one of the first accredited social media certification programs in the world.

Connect with Krista Online:

 Krista.Neher.Pro

 @KristaNeher

 Krista Neher

 @KristaNeher

Want to Work with Krista?

Krista works with a wide variety of businesses across industries and can work with you in a number of ways:

- Keynote presentations
- Workshops
- Breakout sessions
- Strategic planning

- 1:1 Coaching
- Executive training
- Corporate training
- Customized internal training programs

Contact Krista for speaking, training, consulting, seminar or workshops: info@bootcampdigital.com or **513-223-3878**.

Printed in Great Britain
by Amazon